The MYSTERY FANcier

Volume 8, Number 6
November/December 1986

Volume 8, Number 6
November/December 1986

TABLE OF CONTENTS

MYSTERIOUSLY SPEAKING	Page 1
Spade Trumps Unplayed By Jeff Banks	Page 3
The Singular Miss Seeton By Neysa Chouteau	Page 7
Cornell Woolrich: The Last Years (Part II) By Francis M. Nevins, Jr.	Page 11
William MacHarg's O'Malley: Transitional Cop By George N. Dove	Page 15
Let the Public Decide: An Interview with Nicolas Freeling, By Jane S. Bakerman	Page 19
A Gun-Toting Yankee in King Arthur's Court: The Violent World of Dempsey and Makepeace, By R.E. Skinner	Page 25
Further Gems from the Literature By William F. Deeck	Page 27
The Cream of Queen By Frank Floyd	Page 31
IT'S ABOUT CRIME By Marvin Lachman	Page 33
VERDICTS Book Reviews	Page 37
THE DOCUMENTS IN THE CASE Letters	Page 47

The Mystery Fancier
(USPS: 428-590)
is edited and published bi-monthly by
Guy M. Townsend
1711 Clifty Drive
Madison, IN 47250

SUBSCRIPTION RATES: Second-class mail, U.S. and Canada, $15.00 per year (6 issues); first-class mail, U.S. and Canada, $18.00; overseas surface mail, $15.00; overseas air mail, $21.00. Overseas subscribers please pay in international money order, check drawn on U.S. bank, or currency; no checks drawn on foreign banks, please.

Single copy price: $3.00
Second-class postage paid at Madison, Indiana
Copyright 1986 by Guy M. Townsend
All rights reserved for contributors
ISSN: 0146-3160

Mysteriously Speaking . . .

I was just putting the finishing touches on this issue when I received a note from a friend, which read, "I assume you've seen the page Bob [Napier] wrote about you, sent w/ Nov. [**Mystery and Detection Monthly**]." Actually, I haven't seen it, but I'm not very surprised to discover that it--whatever "it" may be--exists, nor am I surprised that Bob didn't see fit to let me know about it. In fact, not letting me know about it makes perfectly good sense from Bob's point of view--since he has no intention of publishing anything that I may write to his "censorzine," there would have been no point in letting me know about it.

This dead horse reeks to the heavens, and I hope this will be the last issue of TMF in which it need be discussed. To keep the record straight, however, I would like to summarize the events to date so that none of us will go away from it with any confusion about who did what to whom.

1) It began when Bob announced that he would not allow the name L.A. Morse to be mentioned in **Mystery and Detective Monthly** because he (Bob) had discovered that Morse had gone to Canada rather than submit to the draft in the Vietnam War.

2) I then wrote a very long letter to Bob, as the editor of **Mystery and Detective Monthly**, pleading with him not to interject censorship into the field of mystery fandom.

3) Bob replied in a letter marked "Not for Publication" that MDM was his magazine, with which he would do as he pleased, and that he wasn't publishing any letters which disagreed with his decision.

4) I wrote him another long letter pleading with him to reconsider.

5) He responded with a short refusal.

6) I discovered from several sources that a number of people had likewise been upset by Bob's action and had complained to him (with exactly the same results--none).

7) Believing the interjection of censorship into mystery publications to be a matter of grave importance, I broached the subject when TMF was revived this summer, quoting briefly from MDM and extensively from my letters to Bob. I was unable to quote from Bob's letters to me since had marked them both "Not for Publication."

8) Bob presented me with a bill for $100 for quoting from MDM without permission.

9) The September/October issue of TMF came out, in which I published every word that had been written to TMF regarding the censorship question (except for a few short items of the "attaboy"

variety)--with the notable exception of Bob's demand for payment, which he had characteristically marked "Not for Publication."

10) Bob responded at last with a postcard which was not marked "Not for Publication"--for reasons which will be immediately obvious to you when you read it in the "Letters" column in this issue.

11) I proceeded to put together this issue, which includes a few straggling letters on the controversy, and was all done with it except for selecting which reviews to include in this issue's review section when ...

12) I received the news I mentioned above, to the effect that Bob had included a "page" on me in MDM.

As I said above, I haven't seen the "page" and I haven't the faintest idea of what its contents might be. I'd like to think that it was an honest recitation of the above events, together with an acknowledgement that censorship has no place in a free society and an apology from Bob to the readers of his publication for having, in a temporary lapse of good judgment, lost sight of that important fact. If that is in fact what the "page" contains, then I want to be the first to congratulate Bob on having emerged from this fiasco with at least some of his dignity and integrity intact. Unfortunately, in light of the contents of the postcard I received from him last week, it seems likely that the contents of the "page" are something entirely different.

Let me reiterate that I have made every effort to be fair to Bob in this matter. I have pleaded with him personally to allow free discussion, and I have repeatedly offered him space in these pages to express his opinions. I have, in fact, published every word that Bob wrote to me which he had not clearly marked "Not for Publication." For his part, Bob has refused to publish a single one of the thousands of words that I and a good many other people have written to MDM on the subject. (Let me qualify that by adding a "so far as I know"; Bob has not resumed my subscription, which I asked him to do if and when he was willing to allow discussion of the matter in MDM, and from that I conclude that his policy of censorship remains in force.)

Important though it is, the question of censorship in the mystery field is only one of many matters which concern us mystery fans, and I think that TMF, having in the past few issues provided a forum for full discussion of that question, should now devote its limited space to some of those other matters. I don't agree with those few people who have said that the matter shouldn't have been discussed at all--which seems to me to be rather like arguing for the freedom of individuals who wish to censor to be able to do so without the embarrassment of being exposed--but I have allowed them their say. That's what freedom of speech is all about. My main regret is that Bob, apparently unwilling to discuss the matter in a publication in which other people share with him the advantage of not having their words and their ideas censored, has chosen not to participate in the discussion--preferring, again apparently, to express his opinions in a publication over which he has dictatorial control and from which he can exclude any comments which portray him in anything other than a favorable light. I can understand how that would appeal to someone with a fragile self-esteem--hell, my self-esteem is almost criminally robust, and it even appeals to me!--but it seems to me to be morally indefensible, so I'll go on publishing the brickbats as well as the bouquets.

Keep on hurling them, folks; that's what we're here for.

Spade Trumps Unplayed

Jeff Banks

Ever visit the idea of a Sam Spade movie series in your daydreams? Have you wondered why there never was one? Let's take the last question first on the good old American principle of business before pleasure.

The first Spade movie, **The Maltese Falcon** starring Ricardo Cortez, appeared in 1931. The one everyone is familiar with, and you know the title, came in 1941. Between them was a comedy version called **Satan Met a Lady**. That is a series of sorts (though with a different actor playing the hero each time, a la those ubiquitous **Hound of the Baskervilles** that most of the actors to play Holmes appeared in), but it is not the kind of series I was thinking of, and neither were you.

One big reason there was no movie series was Warner Brothers. The studio produced fewer series than any other major American studio, and that its most memorable efforts were Nancy Drew (four films) and Mexican Spitfire (nine films) says a lot. In fairness, Warner also released one of the eight Philip Marlowe films, another kind of not-quite series with seven different actors and almost as many production companies involved (more on this one later), and had an even larger participation in the 1960s in the release of some of the later Fu Manchu "series." There were also the Perry Mason series (six forgettable films, two thirds of them starring Warren William, and one Cortez).

The first film version of **The Maltese Falcon** caused no great stir, and therefore no feeling that there should be any sequel. Cortez, like Warren William, was a successfully transformed silent movie actor (though considerably more able). While I have not seen his Spade movie, I have seen about twenty (more or less half) of his later ones. Some of them had him adequately portraying tough characters (not always the heroes), and he probably could have handled the kind of series Warners would have made of Spade. Perhaps we are lucky there was none.

Warren William had the Spade role, blessedly renamed Ted Shayne, in the comedy remake of 1936. Casting Zasu Pitts as a sinister fat woman (a reversal of the Gutman later immortalized by Sidney Greenstreet) is emblematic of the level of comic inspiration of the film. Even a well thought out and well mounted comic treatment of the Hammett materials, as in the Same Spade Jr. (George Segal) movie **The Black Bird**, is unappealing. A Spade series starring William and emphasizing humor rather than crime/detection would have been unappetizing fare.

Which brings us to the John Huston version, very faithful to the original novel, and so well done as to be thought definitive. Cortez had been more physically imposing than Bogart, or George Raft (who had been first choice for the part), but in every other area the film was as close to a perfect translation of genius in print to genius on celluloid as one can imagine.

Greenstreet, Peter Lorre, and Elisha Cook, Jr., made an engaging trio of villains. Mary Astor was an ideal bad-woman lead. But while this list could go on for pages, you know all that already.

So why no Bogart Spade series? Several reasons, starting as always with the fact it (the story and characters, bought from Hammett before anyone had an inkling of what they were really worth) was a Warner's property. Besides, the War mobilized the movie industry for propaganda; Bogart was needed for a number of propaganda films--some few of them, most notably **Casablanca**, became classics. It was five years after his **Maltese Falcon** before he did another private eye film, and that was **The Big Sleep**, Warner's single Marlowe entry. There had been talk of a Bogart sequel as Spade, and casting him as Marlowe was in the nature of a substitute.

The result was Bogey's second-best private eye film and probably on anybody's list of the top ten of that type. But with our 20:20 hindsight we now see that a sequel would have been preferable. Unlike the ending of the novel, that of the Bogart film left all the villains alive, and after five years it might have been reasonable for some of them to have finished prison terms and others to have escaped.

Gutman, Cairo, and Wilbur could have been back in San Francisco to raise money (with some excitingly illegal scheme) in order to finance a resumed quest for the falcon. Any or all of them, plus or minus Brigid, might have simply returned to get revenge on Spade. Undoubtedly other plot possibilities have suggested themselves to you, and your ideas may be better than mine.

Furthermore, as with most film versions of novels, much of the story material in **The Maltese Falcon** failed to reach the screen in either of the three movies. The very visual "G in the Air" chapter and the by-play between Spade and his lawyer, Sid Weiss, are good examples. Certainly the main plot line was worked to exhaustion, but it might well have been possible to build another Spade film around those omitted parts.

Another possibility is in the building up of minor events or characters from the book. Effie was not so strong a character in the film as in the book, and the illicit romance between Spade and his partner's wife/widow might have provided long and interesting plot matter for a sequel or prequel.

Other villains in stories less directly linked to the first are certainly a possibility. Two of the three Op novels by Hammett might have become Spade stories on the screen. Furthermore, the practice was already established of buying series stories (books) about one detective and turning them into adventures of another. This had happened when the first Raymond Chandler story to reach the screen became a Mike Shayne (Lloyd Nolan) vehicle, for instance.

Bogart starred in twenty-six films **after The Big Sleep**. None of us is so fanatical as to wish all these were Spade movies, sacrificing **The African Queen, The Treasure of Sierra Madre** and other such classics. But half a dozen more Spades without sacrificing too much quality (not an impossibility by then even for Warner Brothers) makes a delightful might-have-been.

Nor was that the only missed opportunity. There was never a

Spade series on TV, and, considering what the tube did to other major detective figures, that may be as much of a blessing in disguise as is the lack of a Ricardo Cortez or Warren William series. However, quality considerations have no part in this.

The lack of a TV series was motivated by the same thing as the curtailment of the highly successful radio series. The country's greatest "Red Scare" was just beginning; soon everyone was involved, and Hammett characteristically chose the unpopular side. Radio, already losing ad revenues to television, could not afford the same sort of strong stand on principle that Hammett was taking--if it ever even occurred to the CBS execs to support him. Television, fast growing through its infancy, was even more afraid of offending. CBS Radio summarily dropped **The Adventures of Sam Spade**, and there was never even a TV pilot made.

NBC, which had aired another Hammett show, **The Thin Man**, for a single summer between its long CBS and final ABC runs, took the Same Spade show for a final two years. Those and the other major Hammett radio creation, **The Fat Man** (loosely based on the Continental Op), ended together in 1951, after the Red-hunting had reached an even more fevered pitch. Sponsor loyalty should also be mentioned: Wild Root Cream Oil (one of the "greasy kid-stuff" hair preparations for men) had sponsored **Spade** for the whole CBS run. Rather than follow the show to NBC, the sponsor retained the same Sunday-night time period and ordered the creation of an imitative series that would have no visible ties to the controversial author. The result was **Charlie Wild, Private Detective**, the title character's name being derived from a long-running slogan-jingle of the sponsor. This show did have a TV version, and there the format was changed to be even more imitative--even to the point of having Effie Perrine as Wild's secretary.

Back when the radio show began (July 12, 1946), producer William Spier ordered his team of writers--Bob Tallman and Ann Lorraine--to emphasize that side of Spade's character most strongly displayed in the novel in the chapter entitled "Horsefeathers" (another of the omissions from the movie version). This was the fast talker, glib and slickly sarcastic. To showcase that characteristic, the show's episodes had a definitely humorous bent.

Episode titles like "The Convertible Caper," "The Cheesecake Caper," and "The Flopsy, Mopsy, and Cotton-tail Caper" (the latter being one of those chosen for immortalization on a When Radio Was King recording) clearly indicate the tone. "The Buddha's Tooth Caper," stretched to an hour-long script and broadcast as a special segment of Spier's other major series, **Suspense**, was an overdone satire of the original Bogart movie.

Yet many of the more than one hundred episodes starring Howard Duff, the first radio Spade, managed to be fine short mystery plays as well as being humorous. "The Chateau McCloud Caper," "The Gold Key Caper," "The Prodigal Daughter Caper," "The Stopped Watch Caper," and "The Bluebeard Caper" are five such quoted from memory of what could be a much longer list. Any one of those might have been stretched without too much distortion into suitable length for a movie production. Duff, who went on to a distinguished film and TV career, would have made a superb screen Spade. He would not have been Bogie, not even an imitation, but he would not have had to play a humor-only hero either.

He had been appearing in films since 1947, and when both sponsor and network dropped his radio series he made a career move to the visual media. It must have occurred, at least in passing, to some of the people he worked for that letting him recreate what was already recognized as a classic radio role was an idea with possibilities. But, again, Hammett's name (and characters) would have been dangerous.

The result was that Duff never achieved quite the heights he might have, and we mystery fans were denied a series of films that would have been well received. Even on the small screen, the possibilities that were lost are painful to contemplate.

Nor has this been even an attempt to cover them all. Free your imagination to conjure with me just a while longer. Bob Mitchum, Kirk Douglas, and Burt Lancaster became recognized screen tough guys not too long after Bogie. By the time they would have been considered as possible Spades, each of them might well have felt himself too big to do a series--which might apply as well to the post-War Bogie--but one and all they could have been outstanding Sam Spades.

Perhaps you were thinking ahead of me about that trio, but you probably have not considered Richard Widmark. Visually as wrong for the part as Bogart, and never quite so luminous a star; but, like Bogart, he first won his bona fides as a villain, then went on to delightfully tough heroes. He could have handled the part, he might even have been available for a series.

Back on NBC Radio, Steve Dunne carried on as the new Spade for two full seasons. His voice was disappointingly youthful, and Spade's characteristic cynicism lacked conviction when the lines were read by that voice. He would not have been satisfactory in the Spade role on any size screen, but the seventy-eight scripts from his part of the radio series contained their fair share of possibilities that Duff, Bogart, or some of the other actors mentioned here might have turned into memorable film adventures for Dashiell Hammett's greatest character creation.

The Singular Miss Seeton

Neysa Chouteau

Between 1968 and 1975, Heron Carvic wrote five novels about Miss Emily Seeton.[1] He endowed Miss Seeton with two unusual attributes. She "has this strange faculty, one might say misfortune," for attracting crime and criminals (**Miss Seeton Sings**, p. 36), and she creates remarkable drawings that are oddly revealing about people, events, and situations. Carvic used both attributes, Miss Seeton's strange drawings and her magnetism for criminals, as devices to achieve his goal of satirizing "detective novels in general and elderly lady detectives in particular."[2]

Miss Marple and Miss Silver were his models and he consistently satirized three elements of the Miss Marple and Miss Silver stories. One of the conventions that Carvic sends up is that of the quiet English village. At first read, Miss Seeton's village seems not unlike St. Mary Mead. Plummergen is a one-street village. That street is straight, wide, and tree-lined, hedged by houses, cottages, and shops, some of which are four hundred years old. Plummergen is "not beautiful, but it has charm" (**Picture Miss Seeton**, p. 19). In fact, Carvic depicts Plummergen as the quintessential quiet English village before he gleefully puts all its inhabitants into one uproar after another. The eccentricities of some of the five hundred inhabitants lend themselves to being engulfed in the uproar. The Reverend Arthur Treeves has lost his religion and either lost or never had the ability to keep track of a conversation. Miss Wickes, who looks like a squirrel and hisses like a swan, afflicts the speech of everyone who hears her: whistling s's abound. Sir George Colvedon speaks so cryptically as to speak in riddles, and Miss Nuttel and Mrs. Blaine speak in venom. In fact, the last two create perpetual verbal uproar. Nicknamed "The Nuts," they are wonderfully creative and zestful gossips. As Carvic puts it, "There was little they didn't know, much they speculated on, and a deal they invented about everybody's business" (Picture, p. 27).

Miss Seeton is a newcomer to Plummergen, retiring there after inheriting a cottage called Sweetbriars from her godmother. Further,

---

[1]**Picture Miss Seeton** (Picture), 1968; **Miss Seeton Draws the Line** (Draws), 1970; **Witch Miss Seeton** (Witch), 1971; **Miss Seeton Sings** (Sings), 1973; and **Odds on Miss Seeton** (Odds), 1975. All were published in New York by Harper & Row.

[2]Heron Carvic, "Little Old Ladies," **Murder Ink,** edited by Dilys Winn (New York: Workman Publishing Co., Inc., 1977), p. 105.

she arrives from London with a great blaze of publicity because she happened to poke a murderer with her umbrella. This makes her a perfect target for the Nuts, who give their imagination free rein. For example, Miss Seeton takes an afternoon nap on the day she arrives, so the Nuts decide she is on drugs. So many people from London are, you know. In a later book, **Witch Miss Seeton**, when Miss Seeton's handy woman hangs a bag of berries above the sink, for the purpose of making jelly, the Nuts see the white bag, see that something red is slowly dripping from the bag, and conclude that Miss Seeton has decapitated a baby.

In fairness to the Nuts, it must be said that Miss Seeton gives them and the village a lot to gossip about. As Lady Colvendon remarks, "Miss Seeton's an expert on crises. Disasters follow her about wagging their tails like friendly puppies" (Witch, p. 25). When a couple of thugs are sent to Sweetbriars to kill Miss Seeton, one thug stays in the car and the other enters Miss Seeton's yard. He inadvertently arouses her hens. The hens make a terrible racket, which arouses Miss Seeton. She raps the thug with her umbrella, which causes him to shoot himself in the foot. The hens, the shot, and the subsequent yelps and curses arouse the neighbors just in time for them to hear two more blasts. Sir George shouts, "Got him, by God--a barrel a buttock" (Picture, p. 67). He and his son Nigel hop in a car to go chasing the suspects and end up in a fender bender with a police car. Just a typical Miss Seeton incident.

As much trouble as Miss Seeton attracts, the villagers are quite capable of getting themselves into an uproar without her. When the Nuts persuade the Reverend Treeves that he must cast the devil out of an abandoned church, the villagers turn it into a festival, taking along tea and sandwiches, happily singing militant hymns, until they get to the church and see lights--and more. People--or things--are fleeing from the church, including a goat in human form! They have interrupted a ceremony of the local witches' coven. The witches flee, the village hounds and a few of the villagers pursue, while the rest of the crowd whoops it up with another hymn. The most dramatic moment comes when the vicar sees an extra gargoyle on the bell tower. The time has come to exorcise the evil spirit. "Begone, I say, cursed spirit Come down at once. Avaunt" (Witch, p. 116). If you are beginning to catch the tone of the Miss Seeton novels, you will not be surprised at the gargoyle's reply: "'I'm so sorry, Mr. Treeves,' Miss Seeton called. 'I can't come down--I'm stuck!'" (Witch, p. 116)

By now, it is probably quite evident that another way in which Carvic satirizes the elderly female detective is in Miss Seeton's high visibility. Miss Seeton does not have the advantage of using her little old lady status as a disguise. People may fail to notice Miss Marple or Miss Silver, but Miss Seeton makes headlines. At the beginning of the first novel, when Miss Seeton pokes the murderer with her umbrella, the newspapers nickname her the Battling Brolly.

In the succeeding books, Miss Seeton continues to attract newspaper publicity. After Scotland Yard puts her on retainer as an artist because of her remarkably insightful drawings, reporters begin calling Miss Seeton a detective, in spite of her protestations that she is just an identikit artist. Although a series of articles in written about her in **Miss Seeton Draws the Line**, perhaps her greatest publicity occurs in the fourth book, **Miss Seeton Sings**. Because she had accidentally unmasked a crooked bank cashier, she is called upon to help unravel a bank fraud in Géneva, Switzerland.

She mistakenly gets on the plane to Genoa, Italy. In Genoa, the police mistakenly arrest her. This fact makes international headlines: "Battling Brolly Jailed" (p. 64). By the time the arrest makes headlines, the Italians have learned of their mistake and are showering Miss Seeton with food, wine, flowers, and even a red carpet. Pictures of Miss Seeton and her sheepish but gallant friends also make the headlines. When she arrives in Switzerland, the authorities temporarily lose her again--she is in the V.I.P. lounge, trapped into giving a press conference. The culminating public appearance occurs when Miss Seeton goes to Paris. She is to draw a woman who works in a girlie show. When she gets to the theater, a thief knocks her unconscious and throws Miss Seeton, her handbag, and her umbrella into a box which is then hoisted onto the stage. Miss Seeton regains consciousness just in time to step out onto the stage as "Miss England." Needless to say, this exploit makes the papers, too.

A third way in which Carvic sends up elderly lady detectives is that Miss Seeton does not detect. Not only does she fail to observe subtle details, she refuses to see the most blatant criminal acts. When a gunman tries to shoot her, she thinks his gun with a silencer is a "newfangled toy" and that the act "must have been meant as some form of practical joke" (Sings, p. 125). When a young thug tries to push her off a tower (only to be tripped by Miss Seeton's umbrella and fall to his own death), she doesn't see the death and sees the push only as a case of "a young man knocked into me and I'm afraid I slipped." If she is forced to face a situation that is unmistakably dangerous to her, she soon forgets it or translates it into something different. A riot in a car park which leaves Miss Seeton "shocked beyond words" (Sings, p. 103), in her mind soon fades into "something of the nature of a student demonstration" (Sings, p. 117). Carvic states that Miss Seeton "has over the years perfected the faculty, despite all evidence to the contrary, of seeing her life as she would prefer it, placid and peaceful" (Sings, p. 46).

Her marvelously revealing sketches embarrass her because, as she explains to the assistant commissioner of police, "Imaginative work should only be for the highly trained. Or, of course, again, for the very gifted ..., and recognizing this tendency toward extravagance in myself, I've always tried to suppress it. Though I'm bound to admit that it does seem to have been getting worse since I've been standing on my head" (**Miss Seeton Draws the Line**, p. 41). (She stands on her head because she has taken up yoga, incidentally.)

It is true that Miss Seeton fails to see the truth of her life. At one point she longs "for the peace and simplicity of her cottage in Plummergen where she could potter through the daily trivia" while ignoring "the fact that she seldom pottered and that violence had erupted in the village on three occasions since her arrival there and she herself had been in the forefront of the troubles" (Sings, p. 172). On the other hand, most other people also fail to see the truth of her life. Instead of innocent Miss Seeton, they see an extraordinarily daring, clever, sly operative. Her innocent replies to questions she doesn't quite understand are taken as brilliant verbal thrust and parry. Her accidents with her umbrella are seen as masterful and deadly self-defense. Even Miss Seeton's friend, the reporter Thrudd Banner, switches back and forth about believing Miss Seeton is as simple and innocent as she seems. When her umbrella causes yet another man to fall to his death and Thrudd sees Miss Seeton holding the gun she had told him was a newfangled toy, he leaps to the conclusion that Miss Seeton had shot the man. He thinks, "And she's said it only made a smell. Some pong. He'd let her fool him again with her pretended innocence" (Sings, p. 134). In a later book, he thinks of her, "All very innocent-sounding--as usual--" but concludes that "this man Fingers had been her assignment, that she'd picked his pocket for the evidence, meaning to follow it up, but the fight had prevented her." As for her enemies, some typical reactions are those experienced by a crooked bank clerk that she accidentally exposes, that "she seemed to think herself so clever" (Draws, p. 177), and that she was a "double-talking old witch" (Draws, p. 182). But perhaps another thief expressed it even better: "This devil-woman had outwitted him" (Sings, p. 218). In other words, to quote Carvic quoting Ouida, "To vice innocence must always seem only a superior kind of chicanery" (Sings, p. 60).

Carvic was a devoted reader of Christie's Miss Marple and Wentworth's Miss Silver. It is obvious that he knew them well, well enough to turn them on their heads when he created Miss Seeton, a detective who detects as much as Bertha Cool diets, an elderly spinster who is as unobtrusive and unknown as Jemimah Shore, and an English village that is as tranquil as the 87th Precinct.

Carvic's plot--and he only used one--may be merely a flimsy underpinning for a series of slapstick scenes, and his satire may at times be so harsh and heavy-handed that it kills the humor, but when he wrote of Miss Seeton he used a loving pen, and I have found Miss Emily Seeton a delight to know.

Cornell Woolrich: The Last Years
Part II

Francis M. Nevins, Jr.

About half way through the year and six months or so after **Fright** came Woolrich's next story collection, **Somebody on the Phone** (Lippincott, 1950, as by William Irish), the last Woolrich book of any sort from the publisher for whom, back in 1942, the Irish by-line had been created. Not a word in the book was new: all of the eight collected tales had first appeared in top-of-the-line crime pulps between 1934 and 1940, and all but one had been reprinted in **Ellery Queen's Mystery Magazine** in the year-and-a-half before the volume's release. All eight were well above average in quality-- no surprise, considering that the book's unofficial editor was **EQMM**'s legendary Fred Dannay--and four in particular ("Johnny on the Spot," "The Night I Died," "Momentum" and "Boy with Body") are among Woolrich's finest works of short fiction. If Lippincott's nine-year association with Woolrich had to end, it's good that the relationship ended as well as it had begun.

Woolrich must have had advance notice that the break with Lippincott was coming. Within a month of the publication of **Somebody on the Phone**, yet another collection of his short stories was in print, this time not in hardcover but as a paperback original like the two Avon collections of 1945-46. **Six Nights of Mystery** (Popular Library #258, 1950, as by William Irish) brought together half a dozen of Woolrich's stories, originally published in pulp magazines between 1936 and 1944. Each was set in a different city--New York, Chicago, Hollywood, Montreal, Paris, and a fictitious **ciudad** in Latin America--and retitled so as not only to identify its location but to suggest, falsely, that its action takes place in a single night. The collection stressed pulpiness rather than **noir** motifs and included one story, "Collared," that had been reprinted just a month earlier in **Somebody on the Phone**. The copyright-page credits stated that the final tale of the six, "One Night in Zacamoras," was brand-new, but in fact it was a rewritten version of a story published more than ten years before ("Senor Flatfoot," **Argosy**, 3 February 1940). This was the beginning of a pattern that Woolrich was to repeat throughout the Fifties, passing off old work (sometimes revised, sometimes untouched) as new; and eventually he got into trouble over it. Having been published as a softcover original, and therefore deemed worthless by definition, **Six Nights of Mystery** was reviewed nowhere and quickly passed into oblivion. Today copies are highly prized by collectors.

While these collections were in production, Woolrich was working on his next two novels, which were likewise published about a month apart--one at the tail end of 1950, the other early in 1951--

and in the same radically different formats. This time the paperback original came first. **Savage Bride** (Gold Medal #136, 1950) was Woolrich's first softcover novel. Thanks largely to Fawcett's line of Gold Medal books, a lucrative market for mysteries, westerns, and action novels had opened up for writers almost overnight, a market which was functionally equivalent to the dying pulp magazines and which, from the writers' point of view, had the added virtue of cutting out the hardcover publishers who until then had been raking off an unfair share of paperback reprint royalties. Unlike any other novel Woolrich had written to date, **Savage Bride** harks back to his occasional tales of fantasy, horror, and exotic adventure for the Thirties pulps. Civil engineer Larry Jones rescues a strange young woman named Mitty from her archaeologist guardians, who are keeping her a virtual prisoner. He marries her at once and they honeymoon aboard the S.S. Santa Emilia, which is taking him to a new job in Central America. (Shades of Woolrich's father and his career building bridges below the border!) The love-struck Jones remains blind to all sorts of hints that the marriage was a mistake and that Mitty has something unspeakably wrong about her. Then his bride jumps ship in the steamy tropical port of Puerto Santo and the Santa Emilia sails off minus both Joneses, who are stuck in this hellhole for thirty days, until the next boat comes. Almost at once Mitty is hypnotically drawn to the desolate interior of the country, to the so-called Tierra de los Muertos, the Land of the Dead, that lies on the other side of the last outpost of civilization; and Jones is drawn along in her wake. About halfway through the novel, after a protracted buildup of menacing shadows and pounding drums, Mitty and Jones--along with the planter Mallory, with whom they've been staying, and Mallory's teen-aged daughter Chris--are captured by a primitive Mayan tribe and taken through uncharted jungle and a maze of mountain tunnels into the Indians' lost city in the land of the dead. Mitty, it seems, is the tribe's high priestess, who had been spirited away in a mummy case by the archaeologists a few years before and was brought back to life in the United States. Most of the book's second half has to do with which of the three captives, if any, will be able to avoid becoming a human sacrifice and escape back to the twentieth century.

The plot owes a heavy debt to Tarzan movies and Maria Montez-Jon Hall flicks like **Cobra Woman** and sinks **Savage Bride** to a level way below Woolrich's best work. But if the novel is impossible to take seriously, it's just as impossible to lay down unfinished. Woolrich tries his damnedest to invest the ridiculous storyline with his unique **noir** sensibility. The book begins as any of his suspense classics might have begun: "His name was Lawrence Kingsley Jones. He was just like any man, like you, like me; and yet, this is what happened to him." The protagonist is thrust into the nightmare by chance or fate or God-the-malign-thug like countless earlier Woolrich characters: lost in the dark, he asks for directions at the wrong house and sees peering through an upstairs window his **ange noir**. Woolrich gives us dozens of eerily poetic descriptive touches ("A coppery haze appeared in the eastern sky, like brick dust floating around in the night") and some unforgettable evocations of horror, as when Jones is forced into the mountain tunnel: "The lips of rock narrowed over him, sucked him in. Darkness." There is even a prayer to the absent god as in **Deadline at Dawn**: "Oh, Somebody, whoever you are, be on our side for just this one time." These moments, not the High Camp plot, are what make **Savage Bride** worth reading, and they demonstrate that even in a misfire of a book like this one, Woolrich remains Woolrich, creating dark magic like no other writer on earth.

The hardcover Woolrich novel that came out a month later was his last in that format and unfortunately his weakest and most conventional. **Strangler's Serenade** (Rinehart, 1951, as by William Irish) was expanded from one of the longest novelets Woolrich had written during his fifteen-year prime ("Four Bars from Yankee Doodle," **Mystery Book Magazine**, August 1945). New York homicide detective Champ Prescott comes to spend a month of enforced R&R in the peninsular resort community of Joseph's Vineyard. What he dreads as four weeks of solid boredom quickly turns interesting from more than one perspective: within an hour of arriving, he has struck up an acquaintance with the lovely local artist Susan Marlow and has discovered the body of his fellow boarder at the local roominghouse, dangling from a noose in the attic. It takes Prescott but a few minutes to prove to the satisfaction of rustic Sheriff Benson that the death was not suicide as it appears but murder. The next Sunday morning, while most of the townsfolk are at church, the local drunk is killed in what looks like an accidental fall down his cellar steps, but once again Prescott shows that the man was murdered, and in a most gruesome way at that. After the richest woman in town also dies (and this time it's clearly murder), suspicion falls on the community halfwit, Lon Bardsley. But Prescott is convinced that this whistling idiot is being framed, and he has to defend him from both the local authorities and a lynch mob. Until this point we've been confined to Prescott's point of view, but now Woolrich shifts perspectives and, as in **Black Alibi**, presents the next murders from a variety of viewpoints, generating a fair amount of suspense as we wonder who will die next. Eventually Prescott makes a wild guess about the motivation behind the serial killings, a guess which, if correct, means that the final victim will be Susan Marlow, with whom he's fallen in love. With her consent, he sets a trap with her as the bait. Thus we reach what everything in the book has been building towards, a fifty-page set-piece of suspense, cross-cut in the grand D.W. Griffith manner as the murderer stalks Susan in her lonely house while Prescott, decoyed away from the scene by one of the dumbest ploys in the Woolrich canon, frantically races across the peninsula to save her.

As usual in late Woolrich, the aspects of **Strangler's Serenade** that work well are offset by elements that don't work at all. In order to clear the way for killing Susan, the murderer sends Prescott a phony telegram in the name of his police commander, summoning him back to New York at once and forbidding him to phone ahead and question the order. Although he's in love with Susan, and knows the killer might go after her at any time, Prescott instantly abandons his watch outside her house and starts back to the city, not even bothering to tell her she's on her own. Shades of the Doubt-Authority-and-You're-Damned of Woolrich's Catholic childhood! But to the extent we gag at this idiocy, the suspense of the crucial sequence in the book is ruined. This is far from the only problem with the novel. The killer's motivation turns out to be both unguessable and unutterably screwy. Too many incidental characters are stereotypes straight out of the movies, worst of all being the roominghouse servant Athena, a fat black mammy who rolls her eyes in fright, speaks in Stepin Fetchit dialect, and has no reaction whatsoever when she sees a lynch mob going after a member of another despised outgroup, the halfwit Bardsley. Even the writing is almost completely without the characteristic Woolrich word-magic of beauty and horror. A few scenes are nicely executed--the interrogation of the women closest to victims number two and three, the eerie manhunt at the climax--but the weaknesses in **Strangler's Serenade** far outweigh its strengths. Unsurprisingly, it's one of the least popular Woolrich novels, and, except for book-club and paperback editions soon after its hardcover release, it has never been reprinted in the United States.

When the book was finished, probably quite early in 1950, Woolrich came very close to giving up writing altogether. The reasons behind his silence are unknown, although it's a safe guess that his mother's increasingly feeble health played a major role. Whatever the causes, between early 1951 and the summer of 1958 the only new Woolrich works published anywhere were a pair of short stories. Throughout those years of course his name and fame didn't suffer. **EQMM** and similar magazines continued to reprint his earlier stories. Two of his finest novelets, "Marihuana" (**Detective Fiction Weekly**, 3 May 1941) and "You'll Never See Me Again" (**Street & Smith's Detective Story Magazine**, November 1939), were republished in 1951 in Dell's series of ten-cent paperback booklets, and both little volumes are priceless collector's items today. The Woolrich byline was seen in the credits of a frightening number of live and filmed TV dramas based on his tales--and of Alfred Hitchcock's 1954 classic **Rear Window**. But despite all this apparent activity, to those who could tell adaptions and recyclings from new work it was clear that the master of the haunted word had fallen silent.

Two new collections of Woolrich stories came out in 1952, one in hardcover and the other as a paperback original. **Eyes That Watch You** (Rinehart, 1952, as by William Irish) was the first and only story collection, and the fifth and last Woolrich title, to be published by the Rinehart firm. Its contents and quality were perfectly summed up in Anthony Boucher's **Times** review. The book, he said, "contains the title novelet and two others ('Charlie Won't Be Home Tonight' and--the perfect Woolrich title--'All at Once, No Alice') ... richly representing his best work. The volume is padded out with four minor gimmick stories, which any hack could have written; but you can overlook them, settle down to the longer stories and revel in the skill of the foremost master of the breathtaking this-could-happen-to-me impact."

At the end of the year, the publishing house which had issued reprint editions of four earlier Woolrich books (the collections **After-Dinner Story** and **The Dancing Detective** and the novels **Fright** and **Strangler's Serenade**) and the original softcover collection **Six Nights of Mystery** came out with yet another such collection, **Blue-Beard's Seventh Wife** (Popular Library #473, 1952, as by William Irish). The six tales assembled here had all appeared in pulp magazines between 1939 and 1939, although the copyright page, like that of **Six Nights**, insisted that one of the half-dozen, in this case "Morning After Murder," was brand-new. The best of the lot were the title novelet and the final selection, "Through a Dead Man's Eye," with honorable mention to the very short and uncharacteristic "Humming Bird Comes Home." The others were of at least average grade. Like all paperback originals of the period, the book went almost completely unreviewed, and was unaccountably ignored even by Boucher, who had been championing good softcover mysteries in his **Times** column almost from the day the **[Continued on page 18]**

William MacHarg's O'Malley: Transitional Cop

George N. Dove

William Briggs MacHarg (1872-1951) enjoyed considerable success as a fiction writer for the slick magazines, but his reputation now as a mystery writer rests on two things. The first of these was his collaboration with Edwin Balmer, which produced the collection entitled **The Achievements of Luther Trant** (1910), now regarded as a milestone in the development of mystery fiction because in these stories psychology as an organized science appears for the first time as a method of crime detection. The other was the collection of MacHarg's short stories entitled **The Affairs of O'Malley**, which, according to Ellery Queen, "started the modern procedural trend."

The O'Malley stories began appearing in **Collier's** in 1931, and a selection of them was published in a volume as **The Affairs of O'Malley** by the Dial Press in 1940. Another edition, with the title **Smart Guy**, was issued by The Popular Library in 1951. There are thirty-three stories in the collection, each of about 2500-3000 words.

The significance of these stories is historical, rather than literary. Stylistically, they are decidedly inferior. The formula, for example, is invariable: at the beginning of each story O'Malley, a New York police detective, is handed a case that nobody else can solve or in which nobody is interested. O'Malley solves the mystery, usually by means of common "cop sense," but at the conclusion he is never given any credit for his success. Situational devices are repeated with no attempt to freshen them up. Historically, though, the stories are important in the sense that they constitute a manifest transition between the Golden Age type of police story and the police procedural. Whether they started the procedural trend, as Ellery Queen suggests, is questionable, but they certainly show a clear mixture of qualities of the old tradition and the new.

The Golden Age flavor is nowhere more clearly evident than in the character of the narrator of these stories, who tags along on O'Malley's investigations and serves as observer and interpreter. His place in the story is never explained or made plausible: he is not a policeman, but he seems to have complete access to police business, serving the role of a narrative artifact rather than an integral part of the story. He is almost incredibly dense, in the Watson-Hastings convention: upon O'Malley's telling him about a thumbprint found on a victim's desk in a particularly puzzling case the narrator responds, "Is it the killer's thumbprint?" (p. 155)[*]

The stories are full of other hallmarks of the classic formal-

---

[*]Page references are to the 1940 collection.

problem school of detection. One of them is based on the Birlstone Gambit, the device from **The Valley of Fear** whereby the murderer escapes detection by exchanging identities with his victim (p. 134). There is the Dying Clue, when a murdered truck driver scratches in the highway dust what appears to be a license plate number (p. 188). In another story we run into the Insoluble Crime, in which all marks of identity are removed from the body of the victim, who appears to have come from nowhere and to have been murdered for no reason (p. 239). Then there is the Silver Blaze Device, the dog that does not bark during the perpetration of a crime (p. 290). In this one, by the way, MacHarg makes a demand upon the credulity that is almost too much: having only the little Pekingese as a witness to the murder, O'Malley calls up each of the suspects and lets the dog listen to his voice on the phone. When the Peek becomes excited and starts running around the apartment, O'Malley knows he has his man (p. 297).

There is one other way in which the stories are closer to the Golden Age police mystery than to the procedural tale. O'Malley is himself in the tradition of the Great Policeman, along with Green's Ebenezer Gryce and Simenon's Jules Maigret, in the sense that he consistently solves the crimes single-handedly: in one story he complains that there are too many policemen working on the case, a circumstance that would not arise in a procedural (p. 67). Calling him a Great Policeman is not intended to attribute to him the polish of Roderick Alleyn or Adam Dalgleish. It is part of the formula that O'Malley has the outward trappings of the conventional dumb cop: his speech is the English of the lowbrow, and his cultural level is just slightly above that of Cro-Magnon Man. "Cherchez la femme," the narrator remarks in one case. "Not at all," O'Malley responds, "what we got to do is look for the woman" (p. 3). These, of course, are the outward manifestations. O'Malley is a smart cop who consistently solves the cases that stump the rest of the department.

At the same time, elements of the police procedural formula, which was to be developed in the next couple of decades by John Creasey, Hillary Waugh, Maurice Procter, and others, show up very clearly in the O'Malley stories. One of these is the convention of the Tight Enclave, which represents the police world as a defensive stronghold against the rest of mankind. The policemen in one of the stories have a great laugh about a stupid blunder of O'Malley's, but they keep their laughter inside the department and away from the newspapers (p. 71). Another formulaic element of the police procedural is the recognition of the possibility that a case may go forever unsolved, which is alien to the classic detective story but which shows up in one of the O'Malley stories (p. 94). Then there is the fundamental game element of the procedural story, which holds that no solution, no matter how clever and logical, is any good if it will not convince a jury. At one point, when the narrator expresses the opinion that a jury would have no option except to convict, O'Malley replies, "You're good if you know what a jury would do" (p. 171).

Also, in the spirit of the procedural, the police sub-culture itself becomes part of the ambience of the O'Malley stories. There is the persistent obsession with credit and recognition: at the beginning of each story O'Malley is almost paranoid about the way the establishment keeps turning the impossible cases over to him, apparently determined that his success will never be recognized even if it is achieved. After one particularly brilliant solution, the people at headquarters are all quick to announce that they had seen through the mystery but had not had a chance to mention their solutions before O'Malley did (p. 196). There is the familiar rivalry between departments, as when O'Malley informs the narrator that he has been assigned to a murder committed up in Westchester because the Westchester cops can't handle it and must call on the New York department for help (p. 51). There is the policeman's guiding principle of vigilance, phrased by O'Malley as "A cop ain't supposed to believe nobody, and I don't believe as much as other cops" (p. 118). There is also the policeman's traditional fear and dislike of lawyers: when at the conclusion of a case O'Malley has pinned the guilt on a lawyer he remarks that lawyers have given the cops so much trouble it will be a pleasure to get one of them electrocuted (p. 26). Then there is the abiding danger of police work. "When a woman marries an officer," says the wife of a murdered detective, "she knows this might happen, but now that it really has happened I find that I wasn't prepared for it" (p. 299).

The police methodology in the procedural story is different from that of the traditional police story chiefly in the way in which the procedural cops rely more heavily upon the laboratory and associated technologies than upon the mental processes of the Great Policeman. O'Malley tends toward the older tradition, achieving his most dramatic successes through employment of his unusually perceptive common sense, as in one case in which only the first half of the combination of a safe is known, and O'Malley gets several suspects to undertake to open it, trying random associations of the other two numbers. One of them does it, and O'Malley knows he must have had the combination all along, because the odds against a random selection are fantastically large, but the man's ego was too strong to miss the opportunity to show off (p. 181). O'Malley is also an artist at setting traps for suspects who are misled by his apparent guileless simplicity into making admissions that eventually convict them (pp. 223, 273-274). He shares with the later procedural policemen such pieces of practical intelligence as the trick of getting suspects to open up by passing the word that one of them has confessed (pp. 27, 308), and the expedient of telling where an automobile has been by reading the elapsed mileage (p. 255).

The police lab does get into several of the stories, identifying bloodstains, determining whether an envelope has been opened and resealed (p. 92), and identifying toolmarks on a window sill (p. 101). Microscopic techniques are used in one case, to determine the kind of surface on which a note had been written (p. 227). By and large, though, the role of the police lab in crime detection is considerably less than the skill and knowledge of O'Malley.

There is still one big gap between the O'Malley stories and the police procedurals, a quality that definitely establishes O'Malley in the ranks of the Great Policemen. I am speaking of the absence of time pressure, which manifests itself in the policeman's heavy case load and in the maxim of the procedural tale: If a homicide is not solved during the first forty-eight hours, the chances are that it will not be solved at all. O'Malley seems to have all the time in the world. In the story in which the Dying Clue figures, he remarks to the narrator, "When a guy gets a thing like this that he can't understand there's only one thing he can do with it: He's got to carry it around and every little while he looks at it, and maybe some day without knowing how he's done it, he all at once sees

18George N. Dove, "William MacHarg's O'Malley: Transitional Cop"

what it means" (p. 189). Such a leisurely approach to detection seemed quite at home in the fiction of the Golden Age, but not in the hectic world of Creasey's George Gideon or McBain's 87th Precinct.

[Continued from page 14] format was launched. The collector who owns a copy today is lucky indeed.

Late the same year, a magazine specializing in fantasy and science fiction published the last work of Woolrich's winding-down period. "The Moon of Montezuma" (**Fantastic**, November-December 1952) is set in the Mexico where the author spent his childhood, specifically in the valley of Anahuac where at age eleven he had looked up at the low-hanging stars and realized that someday he would die. To an isolated house in the valley comes a beautiful blonde woman, with a golden infant in her arms and a rosebud pinned to her coat. She is searching for the American husband who deserted her and the baby he had never seen. Living in the house are a wizened old Mexican Indian woman and her darkly lovely daughter, Chata, whose own baby has just died. What the blonde woman doesn't discover until too late is that both babies have the same father. Chata murders the newcomer, buries her body beneath the white rose bushes planted beside the well in the patio, and takes the living infant to replace her own dead son. But the red rosebud comes to life in the earth where the murdered woman lies, and grows in time into a blood-red bush. When Chata tries to destroy the blossoming witness to her crime, she becomes entangled in its tendrils, falls into the well and breaks her neck, under the eye of the moon of Anahuac. Woolrich tries too hard to be portentous, alternating between the past and present tenses for no good reason, punctuating the storyline with touches of fake profundity. ("The roses sleep pale upon the blackness of a dream. The haunted moon looks down, lonely for Montezuma and his nation, seeking across the land.") But at its best the style is vibrantly colorful and generates a mood of poetic horror.

TO BE CONTINUED

Let the Public Decide:
An Interview with Nicolas Freeling

Jane S. Bakerman

The reading public has long since decided in favor of Nicholas Freeling's thoughtful, exciting novels, though the writer himself remained a bit of a mystery. Recently, however, Freeling has become rather more available to fans and critics, giving several interviews during his most recent trip to the States. This article is based on a taped telephone conversation early one morning in October 1985.

Despite the earliness of the hour and the slight awkwardness imposed by the telephone, Freeling was cordial and forthcoming. While his courtesy and thoughtfulness are clearly reflected in these pages, his humor and wit (often conveyed more by tone than by diction) are not quite so evident, even though these qualities inform many comments. Like his most famous protagonists, Piet Van der Valk, Arlette Van der Valk Davidson, and Henri Castang, Nicolas Freeling seems to seize the day with verve and enjoyment, even as he observes, records, and deplores the self-destructive elements in modern life.

******

How do you organize your writing day?
 I start, oh, mostly about eight in the morning ... after about three cups of coffee, and go on 'til I drop, ... which is two-and-a-half to three hours.... I aim for three pages of typescript a day, let's say twelve hundred words.... I try to do that every day through the working week, a minimum of five days a week. I think it's pretty mechanized that way ... the sort of discipline one acquires. It's a sort of professional reaction.

No waiting for inspiration?
 That waiting for inspiration business is, to my mind, absolutely not on. I think that one just has to sit down and **do** it.

Almost as if you were going to a business?
 Yes, very much indeed; that's very much the way I view it....

Do you think and write in English?
 Yes ... yes ... my English is often not very good; other languages get in the way, and sometimes that comes through on paper ... but, well, that's what editors are for, to shift out what sounds as if it were written in French. And when I ramble or when I say silly things, there's a big red pencil goes through it and "Bullshit" gets

written in the margin. He's a very experienced and very reliable editor; that's why he doesn't bother mincing words. We have a very good relationship--first of all, it's a friendship.

How do you get yourself back into the flow of the story each morning?
It's a habit of work, an effort of concentration. Over the three cups of coffee, I've already started to meditate. You know: what did I say yesterday? And what am I going to say today? Is that any good? Is that just stupid? I might make some manuscript notes in a sort of student's exercise book which I carry around with me....

How fully realized are your characters when you begin to use them? For instance, have you written out the early lives of Van der Valk and Castang?
No, no, I don't ... I never have ... It's been always a sort of spontaneous growth, coming more out of an instinctive, emotional source than out of a thought out, intellectual source. But even so, you do have to think continually, "Look, is this character now behaving out of character ... or is it all of a sudden turning into me?

So you don't see bits of yourself in your characters?
I don't try to disinfect it; I try to detach myself from being predominate or intrusive.

About how long does it take for you to complete a novel?
Well, that has varied very much. I'm getting older now, and it takes slightly longer. And I do tend now to write it all twice. There was a time when I used to say to myself--when I was really young and stupid--I used to say, "Oh, I can do it in three or four months!" But, well, naturally, you have more **energy**, more **physical** energy, when you're a young man ... and you have the advantages that a young man does.
But as you get older, I think you get much better, so that what one loses in energy, one makes up for in--well, of course, experience. There's much more resonance in what you're thinking about, much more depth in it. That sounds a little bit pretentious, doesn't it?

No, no, it doesn't ... you mean that you have to go deeper as well as broader?
Yes! You are trying to make this novel better than the one before.... And to make a character develop. For example, there are whole aspects of a character that you realize that you have never touched, or that you have only touched upon very, very superficially. And in the course of the narrative, one tries to look at another such aspect of the character.
Some people don't like this. They say that this holds the action up or whatever, but I find that it is the only way I can work....

Are we talking in terms of, say, maybe a year per novel now?
Yes, very much in terms of a year ... there've probably been a few interruptions along the line there ... so that it does take nowadays about, oh, fourteen or sixteen months.

Do you jot down ideas for future development, that is, do you keep an idea file?

Just the exercise books that I told you about; just the kind of thing that a school child has. And this I have always by me. It's full of all sorts of rubbish.... Well, your good idea in the middle of the night very often looks **horrible** twenty-four hours later! ... but it gets written down because my memory's rather poor....

When you say you do the whole thing twice, is the second time before of after your editor first sees it?

Before he sees it; that saves a good deal of editorial work having to be done subsequently. I wrote several books that I felt quite satisfied with at the moment when I sent them off.... You know, nice clean typescripts, carbons, etc., etc. And then the editor was making a mess of it: cutting bits out, pushing bits that were on page 156 back to page 45 because he wasn't happy with the sequences--stuff like this. So I [now] rewrite it myself completely; then, as a general rule, not much more than copy editing need be dealt with later.

It gives a sense of satisfaction. I don't like to feel that I've turned in a feeble or sloppy job. I want to feel that it's anyway as good as I've been able to make it, and if the editor then feels there's some more work needed, well, fair enough; he's probably got very good reasons for saying so.

Do you keep an imaginary reader in your mind as you work, some sort of audience whom you particularly wish to reach?

I think this is one of the most difficult things about writing, that one is so isolated from the reader, hasn't even any idea of what the reader's like half the time. Like most writers, I do get letters, and they're mostly very kind, very warm letters that give me enormous pleasure because they create a contact. But apart from that, there's always a screen ... you never have an audience in any tactile sense as a musician has, that you can sort of reach out and feel them there....

I think it's a danger that writers suffer from ... tending to look at one's own navel instead of looking outward.

Do fans ever write to ask you for advice?

Sometimes, yes.... They are nearly always letters from women.... It's very seldom that I hear from a man, and I think they are very nearly always letters from women who are past a certain age group. I have had once or twice [letters from] young girls because they were in particular circumstances, you know. I had one young girl who had fallen off a horse and was paraplegic--that kind of thing. There were some exceptional circumstances. As a general rule, I think my public is middle-aged housewives. Well. And a very good public it is, too; there's nothing better.

Do you read reviews of your work?

As little as I can. I get very few reviews, and those generally not at all helpful. They are generally very superficial, and they often show up that the reviewer hasn't even read the book, and also that [reviewers] tend to have prejudices.

It's one of my problems. I'm not happy with this situation; I feel that I should be making better contact with all these literary editors and people like that ... but once again, I think it's one of the handicaps a writer has. I mean, why does a book have to go to review? Why can't you just sell the book to the public, and let them decide whether it's good or not? The third person interposed this way is an irritant.

What sort of satisfaction do you get from writing, as opposed to, say, cooking or building something?...
It's very much the sort of satisfaction that you get out of making anything in a sense. It's very much of a craft sort of thing; there are people who do gardening; there are people who build furniture. I think it's that manual sort of satisfaction that you get out of making a thing that may be very rough, that may be very crude, very imperfect, but when you've done it all yourself, then you feel a certain pride in that. A craftsman's reaction a bit ....

Should we conclude that you prefer novels to short stories, given the fact that you've published only a few short stories?
I've never felt really satisfied with the short story form, to tell you the truth. I've very rarely done them, except in the earlier years when an editor asked me to. Instead, almost always when I've had an idea that's too thin to carry for a standard-sized fiction script, the usual 70,000 words, then I've tried to wait for another idea, to see whether it was going to build up, to get a little cross-fertilizing kind of thing ....

So that they'll join together?
Join together, yes ....

One feels very close, very empathetic with your protagonists. Did you consciously try to achieve that empathy or did it just evolve?
I think it was again this spontaneous, instinctive kind of thing. And for this reason, I often feel that I'm not a crime writer in the accepted sense of the word at all ... that [the books belong to] a more generalized, more traditional kind of fiction. But this is a thing that one doesn't want to get too up tight about. One tries to keep a certain looseness about all this in order to keep a proper balance.

I feel that all these conventions that have got laid down are very old-fashioned and very silly as a general rule. Being shut in by a lot of conventions, this makes for rather flat and pretty uninteresting writing as a general rule. That may sound a harsh and even unfair reaction, but I can't help saying it. I feel that that's the truth....

Do you ever go back and read your own books after they've been published?
No, I can't! I would squirm with embarrassment and horror. I can reread just as long as it's needed, you know, at the proofreading stage, and even this is a very painful and horrible time. I dread it.

What kinds of things do you do for fun?
I walk a good deal, and I have a big area of ground around my house--on all different levels; it's very rough, mountainous ground. This I try to work on in a garden sense, cutting away at it, trying to make landscapes with it. This is a thing that I enjoy very much doing....

Do you consider it unlucky to talk about a work in progress?
I wouldn't talk about a work in progress, no. I'm feeling freer

at the present moment because I just turned in a Castang manuscript called **Cold Iron.** They're [the publishers] pleased with it. They think it's one of the best that I've ever managed to do. And so I'm feeling rather happy, rather--well, I'm pleased with it myself.

I look forward to reading it.... How do you prepare your manuscripts? Do you compose on a typewriter? Write in longhand? Or dictate?
No, I work directly on the typewriter, a big, solid, absolutely old-fashioned typewriter, the kind of thing that one really has to push. It's not even an electric typewriter.

That means a good deal of physical work as well as mental--
You know, there's a hell of a controversy about this: the great word processor argument. Mary McCarthy, for instance, came out very strongly in favor of the 1920 Underwood, and I agree with this. I agree very strongly with this; I think that that rather clumsy, rather awkward-feeling mechanism requiring a certain amount of energy to push the carriage back and forth is part of the tool, part of the craft's design....

Have you ever set aside one manuscript in favor of another?
I think that if one lets a project, once it's ripe, stand over for any length of time, it'll go bad on you. I think that when the project is there in an imagined form, then I think it ought to be written down. If it gets shelved, for one or another reason, for more than maybe four weeks, maybe six at the outside, then I don't think you'll ever get it back. This, I think, is an experience shared by quiet a few writers.

Have you ever suffered from writer's block?
No, never! I don't even know what it means. That is, I've heard about it, but I don't know what it is. I mean, I realize that the miserable thing is that you've frozen up, that you can't put it down on paper anymore, but I can't imagine that.

Do you do much formal research for your novels? For instance, I'm thinking of Gadget **at the moment ....**
Well, that one I was lucky with because I had a collaborator who was a technical expert. He was a professor of physics, and he put it all down in, well, very rough manuscript note form, just four points on an exercise pad, and this I took practically verbatim over from him. And he was in California and I was in France, and we just had a small exchange of letters on the subject. And then once or twice we were together, and there were a couple of big sessions then with a whiskey bottle.

What about researching police methods?
I wouldn't use the word "research" in any formal or any academic sense at all, and to be honest with you, I don't believe in it. I think that it belongs with a different kind of writing. It belongs, of course, to a non-fiction work or a documentary or a biography or something like that; then, naturally, the research is very, very important. But a lot of torn-out newspaper clippings tend to litter up my table, and if I need any **specific** detail, then I might go out and do, well, I guess the word is "research"--for verification, you know: is this right? Have I got it right? That type of thing. No more than that, actually.

How vivid are the individual characters in your mind before you begin a novel? I'm thinking particularly of the young woman who helps Arlette after the near rape. That young woman is a wonderfully live person.

I think that it's true to say that she came just out of the blue. I don't think--I mean probably there must have been somebody that I had seen or looked at at some moment in a shop of this nature and this became one of those buried memories that pop up at the appropriate moment. And you think, "Oh! I thought of that all by myself...." It's true, of course; you're not conscious of any effort at recollection or at synthesis ....

Do you consciously explore certain aspects of human nature--the depths and maybe even the heights?

Yes, I do.... I mean [I engage in] endless questioning, self-questioning, debate. There is sometimes a sense of dissatisfaction at not having got anywhere near the root of the matter--then you always try to hope, well, maybe next time I'll get it better.

*****

And sure enough, next time, he almost always does.

A Gun-Toting Yankee in King Arthur's Court: The Violent World of Dempsey and Makepeace

Robert E. Skinner

"Such as do build their faith upon the holy text of pike and gun ..."--Samuel Butler

"Violence is necessary; it is as American as apple pie ..."--H. Rap Brown

"God Created men.... Colonel Colt made them equal ...."--Old Western Adage

In 1932, when he was writing his last potboilers, Edgar Wallace wrote a book entitled **When the Gangs Came to London**. In this book, American gangsters (carefully differentiated from the British by their slang and a habit of dropping their "ings") came to London and completely discombobulated the British police with their violent methods.

To save the day, Wallace introduced the character of Captain Jiggs Allerman of the Chicago police force. Jiggs carried a gun under each arm and made it clear he was no gentleman. He punched, twisted arms, shot it out, and generally played dirty to save the bacon of the dedicated but hopelessly well-bred British police.

I remember that story because it reminds me of a British television program that has lately made its appearance on the American screen. It is entitled **Dempsey and Makepeace**, and it is amazing to me how much this modern-day program resembles that fifty-five year old British thriller.

A joint production of London Weekend Television and the American Tribune Broadcasting Company, **Dempsey and Makepeace** essentially takes the same stand that Wallace did: to wit, the London Metropolitan Police are simply too polite and inexperienced in the ways of real crime and criminals to be able to cope with them effectively. Enter Lieutenant Jim Dempsey.

As played by American actor Michael Brandon, Dempsey is the quintessential hard-boiled detective. He is tough, uncompromising, violent, and thoroughly professional in the pursuit of running down criminals.

The explanation for his presence on the London Metropolitan Police is, I fear, one of the more far-fetched plot devices brought to the screen. Borrowing a little from **Serpico** and not a little from the late, unlamented **McCloud** TV series, Dempsey, we are told, was just a little too good at his job and ran afoul of the wrong people. To protect him, his superiors sent him to London on a kind of "lend-lease" basis.

Dempsey's presence on the Metropolitan Police Force is to the absolute chagrin of Inspector Spikings, played by Ray Smith (who bears a striking resemblance to American actor Ed Asner). Dempsey's way of charging head-long into a situation, his disdain for regulations, and his (to Spikings) frightening propensity for getting into pitched gun battles makes him a decided pain in the neck for his erstwhile boss.

As if Dempsey didn't have enough problems trying to cope with his new surroundings and the inexplicable ways of the British police, Spikings pairs him with Lady Harriet Makepeace (played by Glynis Barber), a perky and attractive sergeant on his staff. Dempsey and Makepeace, in true Tracy and Hepburn style, get along much like a cat and a dog. They are wary of each other, attracted to each other, and not at all sure that the other is the ideal partner.

Dempsey, for his part, is a thorough-going male chauvinist pig. His feelings about women seem to be that they should stay at home. In spite of the fact that Harriet (whom he calls Harry) turns out to be a competent cop who is capable of bailing him out of a number of tight spots, he can't quite adjust to the idea of being a partner to someone so unmistakably feminine (and, by the way, a woman to whom he is sexually attracted).

Harry finds Dempsey attractive, too, but she is much too stubborn and strong-willed (to say nothing of professional) to ever let him know it. She realizes from the first that she can never let him have the advantage of her, and his purposeful boorishness gets on her nerves more than once.

This is a really unusual television show, albeit the whole thing comes off like you would imagine a Japanese western would. The producers try very hard to make Dempsey a real person, but he is cut too much from the Race Williams/Mike Hammer school of detection. Thinking isn't his long suit. He has gotten where he is by being tough and a little headlong in his pursuit of criminals. He is also violent in the extreme. In one episode he shoots up a bar to get a recalcitrant bartender to tell him information he needs.

It is apparent that the producers of **Dempsey and Makepeace** have been very much influenced by the violence on American television, because that is what they have sought to emulate. In fact, this program is quite a bit more violent than most American programs. The body count at the end of each show is positively impressive. For years, we have been used to the idea the British policemen don't carry or use firearms. Yet on this program **everybody** carries one. I don't know if policy over there has changed with all the terrorism London has experienced or if this is part of the imagination of the producers.

In any case, every program has at least two shoot-outs, with Dempsey center stage. He carries a lethal-looking Colt Diamondback revolver, and he uses it to good effect. Much too good for the comfort of poor Inspector Spikings, who often refers to Dempsey as "that bloody cowboy."

This program says some very interesting things about how the British feel about Americans. Many years ago, D.H. Lawrence said that the American heart was "cold, isolate, and a killer." It was that somewhat darkly romantic view of America that probably made Raymond Chandler's work so popular there. The American detective hero is, to the British, very much a "saint **[Continued on page 30]**

Further Gems from the Literature

William F. Deeck

Following timidly in the giant footsteps of Bill Pronzini, Doug Greene, and Jacques Barzun and Wendell Hertig Taylor, I offer the following quotes, from works both old and new, that may appeal to the reader as risible or curious.

If the right word isn't at hand, pick one that sounds like the right word or sounds like it might be the right word:

"Trout had provided a tray of sandwiches and some old Scot's whiskey and soda."--**Fit to Kill** (original title: **Ways of Death**), by Hans C. Owen.

"Hattie bustled onto the platform and took her place behind the podium."--**Die for Love**, by Elizabeth Peters.

"Stoner was an old ward healer who became a compromise candidate for lieutenant governor."--**A Midsummer's Night Murder**, by Robert F. Baylus.

"She noticed that his right foot was clamped to the floor of the car in a constant breaking action, whereas she was hardly touching the brakes at all...."--**Dupe**, by Liza Cody.

"You do not take your life by **hara-kiri** lightly in Japan. It's only when you've committed a dishonorable act. This ritual form of suicide wipes out the dishonor--at least, that's the esthetics of it."--**The Door Between**, by Ellery Queen.

"There were those who could read more into handwriting than a biologist into a drop of pond water. It was just as well the study of calligraphy was a new science."--**Harm's Way**, by Catherine Aird.

"Get this straight: Mr. Peters is an employee. Mr. Roberts is his bread-basket."--**The Misplaced Corpse**, by Sarah Rider.

"The props department was deserted.... That left Christopher with a decision. He opted for flaunting all sorts of union prohibitions and went searching on his own...."--**Ratings Are Murder**, by R.R. Irvine.

"It was raining. His feet still hurt. The flight from Paris had made him nauseous."--**The Crystal Clear Case**, by Lee Head.

"Greg's been married once, to a hell of a good woman; and a few years ago, he was the unnamed correspondent in a society divorce."--**Edwin of the Iron Shoes**, by Marcia Muller.

"But we must first, while there is still time, exercise the malign being that is Gilles de Rais so that he can no longer menace the world of the living."--**Death out of Thin Air**, by Stuart Towne.

"There were a number of strollers on the median, college-age kids in sandals and T-shirts, young women in stylish gauzy dresses, even a pair of Arab students in flowing mufti."--**Shadow Kills**, by W.R. Philbrick.

"At the first glance, his appearance seemed to strike some cord in the Inspector's memory...."--**The Case with Nine Solutions**, by J.J. Connington.

"There was a series of mailboxes in the foyer and the inner door should have been operated by an electrical locking system, but the thing was out of order and all that was necessary to obtain egress was to push open the door."--**The Gift Horse**, by Frank Gruber.

"Every one was agreeable and we trouped down to the court...."--**The Curious Mr. Tarrant**, by C. Daly King.

If the word doesn't seem to mean what it means, add an adjective:

"It was none of my business, but one fell so naturally into the habit of treating Pauline like a retarded imbecile...."--**Murder in Outline**, by Anne Morice.

"At thirty-six, Rose Winters was a beautiful woman, but she seldom left the house on Silver Hill and the family was concerned that she would become an introverted recluse."--**Winter Roses**, by Lorinda Hagen.

"He was a Don Juan--a Latin lover with a special flair for attracting luscious women and lethal killers."--Front-cover blurb on the Signet edition of **The Delicate Darling**, by Jack Webb.

Neatest tricks of the week:

"Big Brennan, badge pinned to the light summer jacket over his cream-colored shirt, stood with his hands on his hips, gun-butt jutting, and pushed his Stetson back on his head...."--**A Shroud for Aquarius**, by Max Allan Collins.

"She gave me a nasty look from under her eyelids."--"Episode of the Wandering Knife," by Mary Roberts Rinehart.

"Concealed mikes around the room made his voice seem to come from different places...."--**Death out of Thin Air**, by Stuart Towne.

William F. Deeck, "Further Gems from the Literature"

"His frosty gray eyes were like twin volcanoes spouting fire."--**Death out of Thin Air,** by Stuart Towne.

"Fisher, who was an observer of some discernment, noticed under the overcoat a creased blue suit, large black boots, and a pair of pearl studs."--**The Clue of the Twisted Candle,** by Edgar Wallace.

When inscrutable is not inscrutable:

"... Loyalty and honest Oriental vengeance toward the unknown person who had murdered Wong's beloved Mr. Roberts were implicit in his bearing and in his somber, inscrutable eyes."--**The Misplaced Corpse,** by Sarah Rider.

Well, it almost says what the author intended it to say:

"Riley had not yet made the association between Goldberg and the fiasco. But Goldberg held absolutely no illusions that Riley would come to the conclusion sooner or later."--**A Midsummer's Night Murder,** by Robert F. Baylus.

Department of clear thinking:

"I acknowledged the brilliant timing of Mr. Robert's murder; the selection of an hour or two at midday on Saturday when the chance of a complete alibi for every moment is unlikely for anyone who chances to be alone...."--**The Misplaced Corpse,** by Sarah Rider.

"Until he had thoroughly satisfied himself that none of these four had had a hand in the killing, it would be foolish to go off on wildgoose chases in other directions, no matter how promising or inviting they might seem."--**The Man Without a Head,** by Joseph Bowen.

Hisses that could be hissed only by villains:

"He clearly heard the old man hiss: 'If you fail, deliberately or not, or if you decide to play some other game, I'll crush you like a cockroach on a concrete floor."--**Razor Game,** by James Grady.

"I have warned you," he hissed."--**The Clue of the Twisted Candle,** by Edgar Wallace.

Adverbs chosen to fit the context:

"'Are you a pacifist, by any chance?...'
"... Smollett straightened up and shot his chin forth militantly. 'Yes,' he said, 'I am....'
"'And he's one of the officers in the American Peace League.'
"Smollett nodded belligerently."--**Death of a Merchant of Death,** by Norman Stanley Bortner.

On the one hand and on the other hand by a master stylist:

"He looked up and saw facing him a young Italian, a typical gangster. One of those dark, vicious rats, spewed from the slimy sewer of iniquitous abomination, that had cast a curtain of obloquy on the millions of decent, hard-working citizens of Italian extraction."--**Fit to Kill** (original title: **Ways of Death**), by Has C. Owen.

[Continued from page 26] with a gun."

I don't doubt that the American fascination with guns and violence is itself fascinating to the British. The average Englishman can live his entire life without seeing or touching a gun a single time, yet the average American actually owns one (or several).

What is especially interesting about the entire premise of this television show is that an American is the hero. For years the British police have had a tradition of preventing and foiling crime with their brains rather than their brawn. Their books, motion pictures, and television programs have all celebrated this aspect of the British detective. Now, the British, themselves, have created this program that romanticizes a violent American come to clean up the mean streets of modern-day London.

The last fifteen minutes of the average **Dempsey and Makepeace** episode usually ends with a breathtaking chase climaxing in a pitched gun battle in which Dempsey (sometimes with the enthusiastic help of Harry and Spikings) mops up the opposition. As the harness bulls and the medical people come in to clean up the gore, Harry generally rewards our hero with an admiring gaze and even the usually truculent and disapproving Spikings adds a reluctant but approving nod, as if to say, "I don't approve of your methods, Dempsey, but I must admit they get results."

There is something sociologically significant about this program that is probably going to go unnoticed because the sentiments involved are being expressed in a crime show and something of a crime show caricature, at that.

At the risk of sounding like an amateur sociologist, I'm tempted to suggest that even the traditionally sensible British, surrounded as they are by the same terrorists and madmen that threaten us all, are beginning to be tempted by the supposedly American tradition of shooting first and worrying about the law afterwards. This TV program, coming fairly soon after the production of a thoroughly right-wing British motion picture of the same ilk (**The Final Option**) is indicative of the fact that there must be some atypical thinking going about over in the land of common sense and diplomacy.

Of course, this may be purely a presumption on my part, since this is just one program out of many and, after all, we don't know how popular this show is over there.

Still, it would be interesting to know what the audience response to **Dempsey and Makepeace** is over in Great Britain, wouldn't it?

The Cream of Queen

Frank Floyd

Clark Howard. "The Wide Loop," EQMM, October, 1986.

In "The Wide Loop" as in other stories, Clark Howard, the winner in 1985 of the first-ever EQMM Readers Award, throws two basic ingredients in with four secret ingredients to conjure up a potent spell over crime-adventure readers. The two basic ingredients are that the writing is well done to the nth degree, professional and fit, and that the characters, the men and women, like lone separate instruments, some almost in tune, some broken-stringed, make quavering individual sounds. As for the ingredients which I refer to as secret, they are really nothing more than either principal elements of Howard's writing technique or certain outgrowths of his philosophy of writing. Their presence is as obvious as the presence of the basic ingredients, but their special contribution to the entire effect of Howard's stories is not as readily seen, while the significance of the basic ingredients is at once evident.

Of the mystery and crime stories you have read in the past decade, what percent has centered around a character whom you felt was from dull to detestable? One of the four secret ingredients is sympathetic characters, usually two or more to a story, somewhat aligned, but as often as not pitted against each other. Howard strikes a fine balance with lead characters who are truly sympathetic, not maudlin, nor over-good nor over-bad, not supermen. Neither dwelling on nor ignoring their frailties, he places all the emphasis on their common humanity, and writes as much about their relationship to life and fate as to each other.

The second ingredient may seem to be much the same as the first one, but is not at all. The characters' lives are in flux, changing, ebbing and flowing. With no greater perception of their future than the rest of us have of ours, they find themselves enmeshed in situations where they are forced by their own inner-existence (by their own ideas and emotions and thoughts) into decisions and reactions which may or may not be in their best interests.

The third secret ingredient is Howard's telling his stories through scenic passages suggestive of scenes from a play--in length, shifting viewpoint, and in being selected segments of on-going occurrences ich are building toward a future resolution. The passages are ...hosen to disclose all that has gone on between them as well as to unveil the essence of the whole. By using scenic passages to tell stories of 8,000 words, rather than the more common 5,000 words or less, Howard is able to create fast-moving short fiction with the features of a novel.

"The Wide Loop" is told in eleven scenic passages. In passage one, we meet Ed Polk, a modern-day range detective. Polk wouldn't ordinarily take the job of seeing that Dave Flood gets sent back to prison as soon as possible after he gets out, for which the local cattlemen's association has offered him $25,000, but Polk, who has been on the bottle for three years and hopes that with the job and money he can redeem himself with his wife Helen, is afraid no one else will hire him. In passage two, we meet Dave Flood arriving back in town on the Missoula Stage Line bus, just home from prison. We have already learned in passage one that when Dave was eighteen the cattlemen's association had forced his family from their land and he'd started making off with cattle belonging to the association. Dave is now twenty-eight and has been in trouble with the law three times, for rustling the association's cattle, and the next time he goes up for twenty-to-life. He "can't take no more of the pen" and has decided not to bother the association's livestock any more.

Passage three introduces Polk's wife Helen; passage four introduces Dave Flood's brother Duane and his family; passage five relates a plot development; and so on until the resolution in passage eleven. The fourth secret ingredient is a twist on the O. Henry surprise ending, which, to my knowledge, Howard himself discovered. In an O. Henry surprise ending, the disclosure of some bit of new information turns the story on its head. Black becomes white. There is a complete re-adjustment of the known facts because of the bit of information. But in a Howard surprise ending, one of the characters does something unexpected. The story is only turned part way around. Both black and white become gray. For an instant the reader is baffled, confused about how exactly the story has ended; the story flashes back through his mind. Quickly he comes to an insight into the character's unexpected behavior, and the ending only then becomes clear.

It's About Crime

Marvin Lachman

Notes on Recent Reading

The unlikely hero of Samuel Holt's first novel, **One of Us Is Wrong** (Tor Books, 1986, $14.95), is also named Samuel Holt; he's a former policeman who became a television star playing a detective and is so identified with the role that he can't get another part. Still, one can't feel too sorry for him, since he is able to fill four of the five parking spaces in the garage on his Bel Air estate. Holt does a favor for a friend who says he is being framed for a murder he didn't commit and finds himself the target of murderers on the San Diego Freeway. Automobiles and swimming pools take up a lot of time and space in this book, but Holt, the author, finds room for those current standbys of all writers with hardening of the imagination: Arab terrorists. Holt, the series character, is strictly cardboard. Holt, the writer, tries hard, but his plotting is negligible and his ending requires a great deal of disbelief suspended. Writing of **One of Us Is Wrong** in the **New York Times Book Review**, Newgate Callendar said it was "written with style, deftly impresses its characterizations." He also praised its smoothness of writing and summed it up as "neat." I found it amateurishly written and predictable. One of us is wrong.

If you want to know the current state of the Gothic mystery, you might try Judith Kelman's **Prime Evil**, a 1986 Berkley paperback original ($3.50). Erica Phillips, an editor, takes a job as an assistant to a famous writer in Connecticut. As in many Gothics, the estate, Bramble Farm, is eerie and in disrepair; the master of the house, the writer's husband, is strange ... very strange. Sounds normal for the genre, right? Wrong. Erica is pregnant, but rejected by the father of her child. Much of the book concerns her questions regarding whether to have an abortion or to carry the child. Though Bramble is near Greenwich, an exclusive community, none of the local authorities seem especially concerned that there have been several mysterious deaths at the estate recently. Though not wallowing in it, **Prime Evil** has far more gore and sexual perversion than one ever found in this type of mystery before. Gothics (and all mysteries) did better when it was assumed readers have imaginations. The ending is implausible and unsatisfactory, with the heroine saying "Things will turn out the way they're supposed to," whatever that means. If this is what the current Gothic is like, I'm ready for a return to the books whose covers had that single light in the window.

Harkening back to the Golden Age of the 1930's, Patricia Moyes' **Murder a la Mode** (1963; reprinted by Holt, Rinehart, $13.95) is a superb example of the sophisticated detective story, complete with witty dialogue, complex characters, and fair-play detection. If it has any weakness, it is the murder motive which requires a grain or two of salt for acceptance. In this, the fourth of the Inspector Henry Tibbett mysteries, he investigates a murder at **Style**, a London fashion magazine. Though his wife, Emmy, is unaccustomedly on the sidelines in this one, their niece, Veronica (Emmy's godchild), a delightfully scatter-brained model, has a large role.

The world of **haute couture** comes alive in all of its hectic phases from dress design to a major showing. In one delightful scene Tibbett goes to question a designer and finds himself in a studio where "a yard away from his startled nose were—as far as he could make out—about a hundred and twenty exquisitely lovely girls, dressed only in the briefest of panties and bras." (It's really only three models, with an arrangement of mirrors multiplying them, but it's enough to cause discomfiture to the old-fashioned inspector.) The book is not always that light, and there is more meat on its literary bones than in that scene. For example, a cancer specialist's office is superbly described: "If one believed, as Henry did, that buildings could catch and retain some echo of the events and emotions which they witnessed, then this must be one of the most tragic rooms on earth. The measure of human agony, apprehension, and despair which had flowed through it, he reflected, gave it a far better chance of being haunted than had a house which had seen a solitary, swift act of violence."

As that passage shows, Patricia Moyes can write in addition to telling a fine detective story. Also, she showed forbearance, more than an inveterate punster like yours truly would have, by not subtitling this book **The Mysterious Affair at Style**.

There was a time when New York City had very few fictional Private Eyes. Almost everyone knew that the real-life breed in the city spent their time acquiring evidence of adultery, the only grounds for divorce in New York State until recently. Now, as part of the movement of the Private Eye away from California to such locations as Cincinnati, Indianapolis, etc., we have Fortune Fanelli of New York City's SoHo district in Jack Early's 1984 novel, **A Creative Kind of Killer**, which has recently been reprinted by Ballantine at $2.95.

Fanelli is a departure from the cerebral, eccentric type of detective of the past. His one eccentricity is his drinking of Coke, even for breakfast, a noteworthy occurrence in an area where many people use coke. Otherwise, Fanelli generally operates on an emotional level: falling in love at first sight; getting hit on the head when he wanders around a dark hallway; having guilt trips when he questions a homosexual in a tough manner. The book is narrated by Fanelli, who at times reaches a bit far for apt similes, e.g., "she gulped down her despair like unwanted food." He also takes an unnecessary dig at another state: "New Jersey had never done it for me. I wondered if it did it for anyone. I couldn't believe anybody lived there by choice, but probably some people did."

Still, Fanelli's basic decency shines through and makes him a private eye one can identify with and root for. His compassion for the young is especially effective and puts Early in a class with Ross Macdonald, Thomas B. Dewey, and Sara Paretsky, very good company indeed. Also effective is the use of the New York area south of Houston Street (SoHo) and its many art galleries and shops. The story opens with the discovery of a corpse in the window at The Sweatshop Boutique, "one of those new shops in SoHo where all the clothes look like a joke and the mannequins are posed in tortured positions. Maybe it's the weight of the price tags that makes them look that way." This is a book which starts well and finishes strong. What's in between is good enough to make this one of the better private eye debuts in recent years.

I hope that Guy Townsend will not exercise his editorial prerogatives and decline to print my review of his own **To Prove a Villain** (Perseverance Press, 1985, trade paperback, $6.95; $8.00 postpaid from publisher, P.O. Box 384, Menlo Park, CA 94026). Guy's comments about it caused me to move it to the top of my to-be-read pile. (The crash of books toppling as I rearranged them probably registered at least 4 on the Richter scale.) Perhaps unconsciously I had avoided the book before because I knew, from his past scholarly article in TAD, that Guy was anti-Richardist. I have a soft spot in my heart (head?) for Tey's **Daughter of Time** and could not recall an occasion when I enjoyed a mystery more than that winter evening I read it thirty plus years ago in an Army base library in Newfoundland.

Townsend **has** shaken my belief that Tey was correct in finding Richard III innocent and placing the guilt for the murder of the Princes in the Tower at the feet of Henry VII. I still believe **The Daughter of Time** is a marvelously written tour de force, using armchair detection to solve a historical crime, and that belief will hold even if it can be shown that Tey's historical research was faulty or even self-serving. On the other hand, **To Prove a Villain** stands up as a most enjoyable first novel and makes use of the five-century old crime in a different, albeit effective, way.

While it does demonstrate its author's inexperience with some whopping coincidences and one important event that is never resolved at the end, it is a book which can be recommended on many counts. The author's narrative style is crisp and never allows the reader's attention to wander. The plot is unusually clever with its weaving of a modern day crime and a historical one, though some seams do show. The setting, a college campus, came alive for me, and I found the comments on policies and administrators interesting, rather than intrusive. A considerable amount of the book is devoted to the relationship of the narrator and his deceased father. While this could be regarded as extraneous, I found it made sleuth John Miles Forest more of a real person. Townsend's writing about father-son relations was more perceptive and moving than many a "mainstream" novel on the same subject.

I do wish that Guy had been a bit more generous to Josephine Tey and not referred to her as an "amateur," calling **The Daughter of Time** "her little book." Though she was not trained as a historian, her credentials were quite good since, as Gordon Daviot, she was one of the leading historical playwrights of this century. I'm not sure yet whether the traditional or the Richardist view is the right one. I plan to read as much as I can on the subject and, coincidentally, just picked up Audrey Williamson's non-fiction work, **The Mystery of the Princes,** which won a Gold Dagger from the CWA in Great Britain. I'm not sure what viewpoint Williamson has. Stay tuned, Mystery Fanciers, for more on this subject.

Death of Two Mystery Writers

MEL ARRIGHI at age fifty-two on 17 September 1986 in New York City. Though the **New York Times** obituary failed to mention it, Arrighi was the author of ten mystery novels, including two—**Freak-Out** and **The Death Collection**—whose detective is Harrington, a Greenwich Village attorney who has lost his last ten law cases. He wrote several Off-Broadway plays as well as television scripts for **N.Y.P.D** and **McCloud**.

DAN J. MARLOWE at seventy-two on 22 August 1986 in Los Angeles. Dan Marlowe began writing relatively late in life, and his first book was not published until he was forty-five and had given up a successful business career to write full time. He was one of the best writers of paperback originals from 1959 through the mid-1970's and was especially known for his Earl Drake series, published by Gold Medal. **The Name of the Game Is Death** was the first and is generally considered the best in the series (and Marlowe's best book). He won an Edgar for the best Paperback Original in 1970 for another book in the series, **Flashpoint**.

When the bank robber Al Nussbaum wrote Marlowe a fan letter regarding **The Name of the Game Is Death**, the FBI was able to trace him through it and arrest him. Marlowe encouraged Nussbaum's writing career while he was in prison and the latter became a popular short story writer upon his release. When, in the late 1970's, Marlowe lost his memory following a severe stroke, Nussbaum took care of him for several years. Recently Marlowe's memory returned and her resumed writing.

Having been fortunate enough to meet Dan Marlowe on several occasions, I can second the sentiments of his friends in MWA who have written of what a decent, generous man he was.

Verdicts
(Book Reviews)

Robert Goldsborough. **Murder in E Minor**. Bantam Books, 1986.

    As I recall, my letter in TMF 8:4 left off at the point where I was agasted over this book. My most exciting moment was when I first held **Murder in E Minor** in my hands, and I began it with great hope and expectations and with my fingers crossed. Robert Goldsborough's attempt to continue Rex Stout's Nero Wolfe and Archie Goodwin series has to be considered a major project in the genre. His debacle deserves attention.

    Here's the basic drift of the story. After Orrie Cather, with the blessings of Wolfe and Archie, blew himself up, Wolfe has refused to accept cases and stuck to minding his orchids for two years, supposedly keeping Archie around to make sure the orchid records are up to date. Then Milan Stevens, conductor of the New York Symphony, is stabbed in the back with a fancy letter opener; but Stevens, Wolfe and Goodwin learn, is really Milos Stefanovic, a Montenegrin freedom fighter who once saved Wolfe's life. How Stefanovic made the miraculous switch from Montenegrin freedom fighter to conductor of the New York Symphony is never explained.

    As for style, method, and characterization, Goldsborough is the most successful in reproducing Stout's style. He tries to write cute ending paragraphs, however (emphasis on tries), and tampers with Archie's usage of slang, with the result that in places the early chapters read more like an amateurish young Hammett than like Stout. Otherwise, he makes only a few not too bothersome slips and resembles Stout's style more than you might have counted on.

    As for Goldsborough's handling of method and characterization, he misses the one by a wide margin and the other by a great distance. By method, I mean the way Stout arranged actions and incidents and details and introduced characters and clues into his stories, and the way Goldsborough must be assumed to have been trying to do these same things. Here are some examples. Goldsborough drags in main characters more than half way through the book. Stout would have had these characters in Wolfe's office or sent Archie out to hassle or fetch them, probably both, forty, fifty, even sixty pages sooner. It is not until the second half of the book, one half too late, that Goldsborough settles into his case; Milan Stevens (Stefanovic) is murdered in the first half, most of the rest of which is irrelevant grandstanding and "nincompoopery"--showboating would be a good term for it. One high point for Saul Panzer comes when Goldsborough has Wolfe instructing Saul to go to the building in which the murder took place and count the exits (carefully). Using his intelligence guided by experience, Saul counts them (correctly). At the same time Wolfe instructs Fred Durkin to find out discreetly what he can about the hallman who had been on duty the night of the murder, a chore which should have been given to Saul. Fred should have counted the doors, don't laugh. After all, the people who owned the building or worked in it may not have known how many exits there were, and Inspector Cramer with his army of men may not have been up to it. Goldsborough, to pick one last specific example from an abundant category, repeated some of the standard routines at the old brownstone over and over. Wolfe read a book and he read a book and he read and read and read. Fritz prepared a meal, and Fritz prepared a meal, and .... Wolfe said satisfactory and he said satisfactory and he said very satisfactory. It went from satisfactory to monotonous to irritating.

Compared to Goldsborough's problems with following Stout's method of plotting a mystery, his problems with characterization are at least as bad. I will by-pass his somewhat incidental characters, since his ability to depict Nero Wolfe and Archie Goodwin in particular, and the other regulars in the series to a lesser degree, is the item which really causes deep concern for other Stout fans and me.

It is probably not a small accomplishment to get Nero Wolfe, Archie, Fritz, Saul, Fred, and Inspector Cramer right some of the time, which Goldsborough does; but a big part of the time he makes various mistakes with them. Cramer, for instance, calls Archie "Archie" three times within the space of two pages and is so patronizing that he might as well have called him Poopsie--and Archie likes it! Cramer has always thought "Archie" was a swell guy, he says, and he doesn't care for Lieutenant Rowcliff either. In fact, the things everyone, including the murderer, says about Wolfe and Goodwin are heart-warming. Saul appears to have the opinion that the two of them are as good as he is. Fred thinks Wolfe is still the greatest. Not to be left out, Archie throws in a few words praising their remarkable skills himself. Some of this goes on for a full paragraph. One possibility which occurs to mind is that the characters have been through a Dale Carnegie course on "How to Win Friends and Influence People" since Stout's last book in 1975.

They are each and every one so nice. Inspector Cramer, Lon Cohen, Lily Rowan, and the suspects fall over themselves to share what they know with Wolfe and Goodwin. All Archie has to do is ask and they reveal everything, usually with a smile. In light of the mileage they get from what they do know, I am thankful they knew so little.

But, then, I did tend to get them confused with each other. In spite of Inspector Cramer's new-found friendship with "Archie," he couldn't face the speech defect he had acquired if he knew anything about it. He has now begun to sound like, of all people, guess who?--Archie Goodwin. If it helps any, he isn't by himself. Lon sometimes sounds like Archie. And Saul does. And Fred. Fritz, too--no one would have expected it of him. But Archie himself sounds like Lily Rowan or Mrs. Forrester-Moore.

These are some of the errors and excesses in **Murder in E Minor** which bring to nought Robert Goldsborough's grand design. There are others. What has happened to Archie's impeccable taste and almost error-free judgment?--and why does he inconsistently alter between childish behavior, smart-aleck remarks, and acting and talking as he should? The fine nuances are there but trampled on. How does Goldsborough take a monumental genius weighing one-seventh of a ton and make him wholly insignificant in a book in which he is supposed to be the main character? It is kind of like having the sumptuous furnishings for a mansion, and then putting the bathtub in the parlor.

Yes, I recommend the book to followers of the Nero Wolfe series. It has a flicker of imaginative humor now and then and gives rise to nostalgia; and the last forty pages are a substantial improvement over the 150-some-odd pages which precede them. Regardless of the esteem you have for Rex Stout before reading it, after reading it you will have a truer appreciation of what he could have done but avoided in more than seventy stories about Nero Wolfe and Archie Goodwin.

Goldsborough's experience may be a sad lesson, that those who would fain wear Rex Stout's crown may find that it changes to a different size than fits their head. Still, I hope he has the temerity to do it again. What I wouldn't give for a really outstanding Nero Wolfe novel I haven't read! (Frank Floyd)

Bill Crider, **Too Late to Die.** Walker, 1986, 183 pp., $14.95.

Dan Rhodes, sheriff of Blacklin County, Texas, usually handles drunks, minor thefts of beer and cigarettes from a small community grocery, and other normal day-to-day crimes of a small town. It's re-election time as this book opens, and Rhodes' flashy opponent isn't above pulling a few dirty tricks.

Complicating the situation for Rhodes even more is the brutal murder of Jeanne Clinton, a young housewife recently married to an older man. Rumor has it that Jeanne was overly friendly with several men in the community. As Rhodes unravels this complicated case, he uncovers more than he wanted to in the little town of Thurston (population 408, and all of them seemingly with a few secrets). Following some dogged detection and a violent encounter or two, Rhodes solves the mystery, and the solution proves to be a genuine surprise.

In addition to a solid mystery, Crider's novel gives us an absolute accurate and often very funny account of life in a small Texas town. Without ever lapsing into stereotypes, the author peoples his book with colorful, engaging characters. Having come from a small town in Texas, I can vouch for this novel's authenticity. For a first novel, **Too Late to Die** is exceptional and leaves us looking forward to the return of Sheriff Dan Rhodes. (L.J. Washburn)

Lee Martin. **Too Sane a Murder.** St. Martin's, 1984; Dell, 1986; 184 pp., $2.95.

In **Too San a Murder**, Lee Martin has created one of the most interesting characters I've encountered recently in mystery fiction. Olead Baker is twenty-six years old, a former mental patient, who is maybe cured and maybe not. The only thing Fort Worth police detective Deb Ralston knows for sure is that five members of his family have been brutally murdered and Olead is the chief suspect. He is either an extremely likable victim of a frame-up, or one of the most cunning killers Detective Ralston has ever encountered.

With a set-up like this, it's a shame Lee Martin doesn't do more with this novel. Except for Olead Baker, the characters are flat and colorless, and, beyond a few perfunctory references, no use is made of the Texas setting. This is one of the most anonymous books I've read in a long time. The plot has several holes (I find it hard to believe that a wife wouldn't know the names of her husband's partners in a business deal), and the ending is overly dramatic to the point of being hokey.

And yet ... somehow Martin keeps the reader turning the pages. It's hard not to get caught up in Olead's problems. Despite its weaknesses, **Too Sane a Murder** shows promise, and if there is a second book in the series I'll probably give it a try. (L.J. Washburn)

Samuel Holt. **One of Us Is Wrong.** Tor Books, 1986, 311 pp., $14.95.

Samuel Holt is an actor who used to play a private eye on television, and before that he was a cop in real life, and as this book opens, he finds himself the target of several mysterious individuals who want him dead. Naturally enough, Holt tries to find out why someone wants to kill him, and he winds up involved in a case involving murder, kidnapping, and international terrorism, not to mention various colorful show-business types.

Obviously, Samuel Holt is not the real name of this book's author. I have my suspicions about his real identity, but whoever wrote **One of Us Is Wrong** has done a fine job. This is more of a suspense novel than a straight mystery, and the pace rarely lags. The characters are good, especially Holt himself, who is generally likable, tough when he needs to be, and human enough to foul up more than once in the course of a complicated case. The Hollywood background rings true most of the time. Holt the author paints his film and TV people as pretty bizarre in some cases, and that may well be the way it is, since according to the dust jacket he lives part of the time in Bel Air. Or that may be just part of the fantasy, too.

At any rate, **One of Us Is Wrong** is good, solid entertainment. (L.J. Washburn)

Kate Gallison. **Unbalanced Accounts.** Little, Brown, 1986, 128 pp., $14.95.

Unbalanced Accounts is obviously Kate Gallison's first novel. The main character is a private detective named Nick Magaracz. He once made fair money on adultery cases but the laxer divorce laws made that impossible. It's a wonder how he made any money at all. He wonders around muddling through this case until it just solves itself.

Even though Kate Gallison has some unusual supporting characters, they were just a little unbelievable. There was a bag lady who painted herself white and wore a black wig while selling dirty balls of yarn as hats to the people she used to work with in the bookkeeping unit of the State. Also there was a stoned manager of the Boardwalk View Rest Home and his delinquent sons who enjoy cutting up people with a chain saw.

The detective's job is to find out who stole 375 missing checks from the Department of Mental Rehabilitation in Trenton. As a mystery, this book is an amateur's attempt. The thief was exposed before the halfway point of the book was reached, and as soon as someone was killed the reader knew who did it. The real mystery was how many wrong paths the detective could take without stumbling onto the culprits.

Kate Gallison does have talent, but **Unbalanced Accounts** and its "Dedicated Unclaimed Journal" isn't where it lays. (L.J. Washburn)

Peter O'Donnell. **Dead Man's Handle.** Mysterious Press, 1986, 235 pp., $15.95.

Modesty Blaise, the seemingly indestructible heroine created by British thriller writer Peter O'Donnell, has had a curious career in this country. The novels featuring her have been in and out of print many times, and for several years her exploits were only available in imported British editions. Collections of the comic strips where Modesty and her companion Willie Garvin first appeared are also available, but not easily. From the first, though, there has been a devoted group of fans in the United States, always eager for Modesty's next appearance.

She's back in the newest O'Donnell novel, **Dead Man's Handle**, and, like all the other books, it is fun.

Opening with a flashback to the days when Modesty and Willie Garvin first met, the story proceeds quickly to the present time. This time, instead of being recruited for some intelligence mission by Sir Gerald Tarrant, Modesty and Willie have to act primarily in self-defense. Through sheer bad luck, an insane master criminal named Brother Thaddeus Pilgrim believes them to be a threat to one of his master plans and so launches a campaign against them that threatens to be the death of both.

This novel is not quite up to the level of some of the previous books in the series. O'Donnell has always ben known for his colorful characters, especially villains, but some of the characterization in this book is just too broad. The ending is also a bit anticlimactic; Modesty and Willie don't really get to do enough. Overall, though, the book is enjoyable and fast-paced, and definitely worth a look for all the fans of Modesty Blaise. (James M. Reasoner)

Lillian O'Donnell. **Casual Affairs.** Putnam, 1985.

This is the tenth in the series of police procedurals featuring Norah Mulcahaney, whom we first met as a young uniformed police officer on the New York force back in 1972. As a result of some very skillful handling by Lillian O'Donnell, the series has gained a strongly committed crowd of fans who have followed Norah through her professional development and her private tragedy and who are happy to learn, in **Casual Affairs**, that she has finally attained her long-deserved promotion to Detective Lieutenant and that she is adjusting to the death of her husband, Joe Cappretto.

O'Donnell has done so well in the accurate portrayal of police life and police methods and in the development of her main characters that we are likely to forget that she is one of the best constructionists now working in the mystery field. As a rule, her mysteries are no deeper or more perplexing than most, but she has developed considerable skill in her ability to move the story along so that the book has the power to grip the reader and hold him. In **Casual**

Affairs, for example, she uses the device of the suspended plot, introducing what sounds like a very mysterious set of affairs in the Prologue, then dropping it and moving into something apparently quite different in Chapter One. This can be a frustrating tactic if not properly handled, but O'Donnell is skillful at moving the reader along on one story line while making him glance backward to see whatever happened in the other one. The process of convergence begins unobtrusively, with the almost coincidental appearance in the second plot of a name the reader has already met in the first one, then a hint that the cases may be related, and, in due time, a complete merger of the two plots. This kind of construction makes for terrific suspense, because the reader finds himself pushing the author to get on with it and bring those stories together.

In a more conventional frame of reference, O'Donnell also shows respectable skill in her handling of clues. The use of the hinted or suggested clue is noteworthy in the main plot, which centers around the question of whether Christina Isserman is the victim of a coma purposely induced by her husband (the reader will not miss the parallel with the Von Bulow case) and the possibility that Christina may be faking coma for her own purposes. For a long stretch the reader is the only one aware of this second possibility, as the result of hints like "Nobody noticed as Christina's eyelids flickered" or "there was a subtle difference" in her appearance a few pages later. As a consequence of these suggestions, the reader is ready for the apparent hallucinations of Walter Isserman, a series of episodes that would be merely confusing without the advance preparation. Besides these hinted or suggested clues, O'Donnell employs the standard array of informational clues (Walter Isserman's financial condition is shaky), inferred clues (someone is obviously lying), and deliberately concealed clues (Norah explains her plan, but the reader is not told what it is).

With such deft management of suspense, we cannot help wondering why, during the latter two-thirds of the story, O'Donnell resorts to the device of The Bomb, the big surprise for which there has been no preparation, which she drops with fearsome regularity at the end of almost every chapter. This is a favorite tactic of less gifted writers, but it soon wears thin, and we may question its use by a writer who has not found it necessary in the earlier stories in the series.

It has been pointed out many times that the police procedural need not be a humdrum story, a point that O'Donnell has well proved in her ability to make this series as exciting as any private-eye saga. She demonstrates in **Casual Affairs**, as a matter of fact, that the procedural format can be used to advantage in the development of suspense, particularly the procedural emphasis on the private lives of the police involved. Thus O'Donnell, having suggested one mystery in the Prologue and started another in Chapter One, can safely put both of them on the back burner and turn to the account of Norah Mulcahaney's promotion in Chapter Two, confident that the loyal reader is by now as interested in Norah as in murders and solutions. (George N. Dove)

Richard S. Prather. **The Amber Effect**. Tor Books, 1986, 308 pp., $12.95.

The ingredients of today's private-eye fiction are brooding and corruption, mangled relationships and a soiled world. But there was a time when, if you picked up a PI book by one particular writer, you'd be grabbed by plot situations wild and woolly as a bighorn ram, by characters straight off the nut tree--including a bevy of nubile bubbleheads sans clothes or sexual inhibitions--and by narrative and dialogue eccentric enough to pop the eyeballs. For this particular writer the private eye novel wasn't a Film Noir in prose, it was a hoot, no more believable or substantial than a comic book but outrageously, bawdily funny while it lasted. His name was Richard S. Prather and his principal character was Shell Scott, a big ex-Marine PI with the white hair cut Camp Lejeune style and the angular eyebrows and the Cad convertible and the tropical fish. Scott was the first major private eye whose adventures were published as paperback originals, and roughly 40,000,000 copies of those escapades were sold between his debut in 1950 and the mid-1970s. Then, for reasons too complicated to go into here, Prather shut down his word factory. The good news is that production has started up again--this time in hardcover--and that none of his inspired looniness has been lost.

Prather plots defy summary. Suffice it to say that **The Amber Effect** kicks off with Scott finding the doorway of his L.A. apartment graced by an undraped lovely who is both the winner of the Miss Naked California contest and the target of a gaggle of hit men, including a human clam, an ex-Rams linebacker, and a half-senile gun-for-hire known in the trade as One Shot. In time Scott finds the connection between the lady and a weirdo scientist who, before he was murdered, invented something potentially worth billions. All trails lead to a pair of unforgettable wacked-out action scenes where, without a gun and assisted only by several three-dimensional holograms of himself, Scott takes on the entire cast of bad guys. **The Amber Effect** isn't way out there in the stratosphere with alternative classics like Prather's 1964 **The Trojan Hearse**, but-- insane story-line, juvenile double entendres, Fifties mammary fixations, and all--it's a **tour de farce** of the sort no one in the world but this particular writer could have turned out, and it's wonderful to have him back at work. (Francis M. Nevins, Jr.)

Anthony Berkeley. **Trial and Error**. New York: Doubleday, Doran, 1937; Pocketbook Edition, 1943.

Older lovers of the long, leisurely mystery will surely recall **Trial and Error** with fondness. Perhaps a review will win some younger readers away for a while from the brisk, hasty, and, alas, shallow mysteries which are so often presented to readers today. The titles of the divisions of this book are themselves indicative of the pleasures within. They begin with a Prologue and end symmetrically with an Epilogue. In between there is a Picaresque, a Transpontine, a Detective, a Journalistic, and a Gothic segment.

The hero of all this creativity is Mr. Lawrence Todhunter, who, having come to full maturity without becoming encumbered with wife and children, suddenly learns that he has an aneurysm which will carry him off within a few months. Todhunter has a comfortable private income, a housekeeper who cossets him, a conscience which sends him to do volunteer work in a children's clinic once a week, a taste for classical music, and a small coterie of middle-aged gentlemen friends. By way of occupation he writes a review of some suitable biographical or historical volume for the **London Review** most weeks. He is an unassuming man with a wry sense of humor. Until this disastrous news he has lived a quiet but satisfying life. Now the question arises in his mind, "How shall I best live the short rest of my life?"

Not wanting to burden his friends with an embarrassing knowledge of his mortality, yet wanting advice, he puts the problem to them abstractly. During some discussion after dinner, his friends--an old soldier, the **Review** editor, a clergyman, and amateur detective Ambrose Chitterwick--come to the conclusion that the best use of a few months of life would be to murder someone whose removal would release some people from pain in their lives and bring about happiness. The friends, perhaps needless to say, were in a bantering mood. But Todhunter took them quite seriously and started out to find a murderee.

An appropriate candidate turned up in the offices of the **London Review** in the person of a new managing editor who was firing their best men. Todhunter determined that the man had no redeeming qualities and that his death would only be a benefit to his friends and to the **Review** itself. He was about to work out a practical method when another fate overtook the person in question.

At that he decided to stop. Murder, he thought, was not his metier. With his only candidate for murderee removed, he settled back to live out his life as quietly as he has lived his first fifty-one years. Fate, however, had not done with him. Fate came in the shape of Nicholas Farroway, an author of popular fiction; they met in an auction house where Todhunter was browsing, and Farroway took him home to his mistress's flat for tea, under the mistaken impression that Todhunter was a very rich man and worth cultivating. Thus began the most exciting part of Todhunter's life. If he had not met Farroway by chance that day, he would not have met Jean Norwood, actress-manager, or Felicity Farroway, Nicholas's daughter and budding actress, or Mr. Budd, of the Sovereign Theatre, or a good many others, and the course of his and many other lives would have been very different. Todhunter would never have been involved in a murder case, never have handled a gun, never have been in jail, never have been the center of a cause celebre. Strangely enough, the aneurysm held up through all the excitement, until Todhunter himself was ready to die. Just so can authors arrange the lives, and deaths, of their characters.

Probably conversations with a convicted murderer in the death cell never were much like those reported in the latter chapters of this book. Certainly they'd not be much like them today. But then, this book is not concerned with realism. Todhunter's whole project is a dream, a romance, a fantasy of an aging man whose life has been dull, if pleasantly so, and looks to continue that way. So we as readers grant him a willing suspension of disbelief, allow him the thrills of an exciting last few months, and cheer him on to an ultimate victory. At least I do!

What a book for the sleepless night, the rainy weekend in the country, the snowed-in days, the hours when there's nothing good on television, the convalescence from some none-too-serious illness. Lawrence Todhunter, wending his bewildered way through encounters with passionate lovers, wives done wrong, actresses who act off the stage as well as on, barristers, solicitors, and policemen, and bending them all to his will, is a veritable Walter Mitty of the mystery, only more so, because Todhunter's fantasies do, in a manner of speaking, come true. (Maryell Cleary)

Jonathan Gash. **The Tartan Sell.** St. Martin's, 1986, 186, $14.95.

A Lovejoy novel is close to pure entertainment. It is cover-to-cover romp with Lovejoy chasing dastardly criminals, being caught by lecherous women, and feeling acutely the pains from risking life and limb in his adventures. Once we get to know Lovejoy, we realize what a simple bloke he is. He is uncompromising in seeking justice, unrestrained in making a fast buck from faking antiques, unfaltering in disdain for the police, uncontrolled in reacting to authentic antiques, undiscriminating in love-making, and undignified in fearing pain. None of these reactions are within Lovejoy's control. It can be said that Lovejoy is pure of heart.

The Tartan Sell follows the pattern of the previous Gash books and is, thus, filled with Lovejoy loving the antiques, sex, and justice. The scene is Scotland and is magnificent in natural flavor. The story begins, however, in Lovejoy's East Anglia, where the murder of a lorry driver occurs. Lovejoy is considered responsible, since he had planned to meet the unlucky driver who was delivering an antique. After some time in jail and then some time in a traveling carnival, Lovejoy flees to Scotland following traces that might lead to the murderer or murderers and quite possibly to the source of some fine antique "reproductions." Lovejoy assumes an alias and attempts to join the strange old family of McGunns.

Another predictable and wonderful part of a Lovejoy novel is the elaborate scam that leads to the undoing of the guilty. This one is a giant antiques auction. Lovejoy teaches the McGunns some tricks they had not thought of, arranges for his trusted criminous buddies to participate, and entices dealers (**all** crooked according to our hero) to come. Still, Lovejoy must face more trouble but does so unquestioningly to get to the many sources of the wicked deeds. (Martha Alderson)

Anne Morice. **Dead on Cue.** St. Martin's, 1985, 192 pp., $12.95.

The title and the jacket art of **Dead on Cue** are more to let readers know that **this** Morice novel has plenty of inside stage-talk than to relate to the story. There is also much humorous parody of publishing mystery novels as the opening is at the Alibi Club, a version of the Golden Age's Detective Club. The Alibi Club, however, has come to include science fiction writers because the "old fashioned classic detective novelists" are "getting thinner on the ground."

One of the prolific members of the Alibi Club, William Montgomerie, has just died, and another, Myrtle Sprygge, who feels she may have the ability to predict murder, dies soon afterwards but not before confiding in Tessa Crichton that one of her stories may have been stolen. In fact, Tessa, the cheeky amateur sleuth, recognizes one of Myrtle's plots in a film in which she has been chosen to star. This situation allows Morice to present witty dialogue and many insider's scenes for both worlds she knows so well-writing and acting.

When another death occurs, one which is clearly a crime, Tessa is off and running pursuing her avocation, solving murders.

Those who are on Tessa's list of suspects include novelists and film people, hangers-on, and relatives of the deceased, including new neighbors of Tessa's professionally eccentric cousin Toby. There are many loose ends to tie, and the final result is a satisfying weaving together of them all. This is vintage Morice--a clever story, believable characters with believable motives, a nice splash of theater atmosphere, and the trusty continuing case--proving that this classic detective novelist is keeping the ground from becoming too thin. (Martha Alderson)

Anne Morice. **Publish and Be Killed.** St. Martin's, 1986, 192 pp., $12.95.

In the latest word play on the "publish or perish" adage, Anne Morice weaves a tale of mishap, murder, and family politics spurred by the possibly damning publishing of a set of old family letters. It's the sort of intrigue Tessa Crichton loves. She examines minutely the lives of the offspring (three legitimate, three otherwise) of the deceased celebrated actor, Sheridan Seymour. This examining involves some of Tessa's acting talent but mostly her incessant inquisitiveness. Morice often uses a family as her circle of suspects, and the more complicated their relationships the better. In **Publish and Be Killed** she presents enough complexity to challenge the amateur detective but not so much to be confusing to the readers.

Because Seymour's granddaughter from the otherwise side of his progeny is now married to an associate of Tessa's husband, Robin, all of this snooping is actually to Robin's benefit. For a change, Robin is pleased by her interest in the events, although he reverts to patronizing sarcasm by the time Tessa has worked out a very elaborate scheme.

This latest novel illustrates why critics say Morice writes "mysteries of manners." Most of Tessa's sleuthing takes place at dinner parties, tea, or on the telephone. All is resolved, as usual, at cousin Toby's Roakes Common home in the country, "where everything is in its right place and the old values still count." This brings a pleasant resolution to Morice's twenty-first Tessa Crichton mystery of manners. (Martha Alderson)

The Documents in the Case
(Letters)

From Robert S. Napier, 14411 S. C St., Apt. C, Tacoma, WA 98444:

[Well, folks, Bob finally decided to send me a piece of correspondence which was not marked "Not for Publication." In fact, it was clearly intended to be read by as large an audience as possible since it was in the form of a postcard. Here it is, in its entirety:]

Two facts:
1) Every letter I sent to a correspondent was 100% original. I didn't use form letters and I didn't use boilerplate. Your suggestion to the contrary is cheap and venal.
2) When I want legal advice about copyright laws from a guy who flunked his bar exam I'll ask you. Until that time, save your breath.
[Signed:] Cap'n Bob

[My "suggestion," to which Bob refers in his first point, was as follows:

I seriously doubt that Bob did in fact write a different long letter to every person who complained. He has a computer, and he probably used the same latter [sic] in every case, altering it slightly to meet the exact nature of the different complaints which he received. Any sensible person, confronted with the need to say the same thing to a large number of people, would have done that.

I hereby publicly apologize for having suggested that Bob was a sensible person. This entire episode has produced an abundance of evidence to the contrary, and I am at a loss to explain how I could, in the face of all that evidence, have been so foolish as to suggest that Bob was sensible. I assure the public at large and Bob in particular that I won't make that mistake again. I am further at a loss to understand how my suggesting that Bob had acted as "any sensible person" would have acted is in any way cheap or venal, but it is quite clear at this point that words don't mean the same thing to Bob that they do to those of us who are constrained by the definitions which we find in our dictionaries, so I'll let it pass.

I am sufficiently annoyed by Bob's ad hominem second point to reiterate a few points that I have previously made about my law school experiences and to add a few new ones. To begin with, the law school program in which I was enrolled—designed for people like myself who have jobs and must attend school at night—is intended to be completed in four years, yet I, by going to school year round and taking overloads, successfully completed the program in only three. To graduate with the class ahead of me I had to attend summer school this past summer, as a result of which I did not take my last final examination until 10 July 1986. Those people who finished their classes in May were able to prepare for taking the bar examination by enrolling in bar review courses, about which a few words of explanation are in order.

Last time I looked, there were still one or two states which allow graduates of accredited law schools within their borders to be admitted directly to the state bar without having to take a qualifying examination (South Dakota comes to mind), but most states now require that individuals wishing to be admitted to their bars take and pass qualifying examinations. These bar examinations cover the full range of the law, and it is not possible for any law student, in the three or four years that he spends in law school, to take courses in every one of the areas of law which may be covered on the bar exam. For that reason, and because the bar exam covers subjects which students have taken one, two, or three years earlier, it is common—indeed, well-nigh universal—practice for law school graduates to take bar review courses immediately before they take the bar examination. These courses, which meet for four to six hours a day, five days a week, and run from five to ten weeks, are intended brush up the student's memory of courses which he took several years before and to give him at least some grounding in courses which he was not able to fit into his law school curriculum.

Now, in May, June, and July, when the May graduates were busily attending bar review classes and otherwise preparing themselves to take the July bar examination, I was attending school four nights a week taking the last two courses that I needed in order to graduate in August. I took my last final examination on Thursday night, the tenth of July. (It was in Federal Estate and Gift Tax and, as I learned only a couple of weeks ago, I received the book award for having achieved the highest grade in the class.) I then had six days to prepare myself to take the Indiana State Bar Examination, which was to be given Thursday and Friday of the following week, 17 and 18 July. I had been advised by my professors to wait until February to take the bar examination, which would have allowed me to take the bar review course and would have given me some time to study, but I decided that there was at least a chance that I could pass the exam without studying for it, so, figuring that I had nothing to lose but a few hundred dollars and a week's worth of sleep, I went ahead and took it. And, as it turned out, I almost passed. A grade of 70% was required to pass, and I turned in a 65.6%—which I thought then and still think was a fairly respectable showing under the circumstances.

So, while I would have preferred to have passed the bar exam on my first try, I don't regard my failure as anything to be embarrassed about. It's not as though I was pretending to be something that I am not, or laying spurious claims to titles which I have not earned. If I were, then I'd have something to be ashamed of. But I'm not going to hang my head over not having passed an examination that I had no opportunity to study for. Sorry, Cap'n Bob.]

From Bill Gault, 482 Vaquero Lane, Santa Barbara, CA 93111:

The Documents in the Case (Letters)   49

    Regarding your feud with Bob Napier and your request for
contributions on this sordid subject, I admire the boys who went to
Vietnam and despise the bastards who sent them.
    As for those who went to Canada, I would have to know why
they went and I am not a mind reader.
    I served in the 166th Infantry in our last moral war--while
Rambo Ronnie Reagan decided to stay close to Hollywood and his
poolside martini and make training films.
    Hell has no fury like a non-combatant.
    And now they have fought and bled, and the Vietnam vets are
forgotten. How soon the avenger citizens forget!

From R. Jeff Banks, P.O. Box 13007 SFA Sta. Nacogdoches, TX
75962:

    Your comeback, the magazine's comeback, was an impressive
one. I would have written sooner to applaud "The Return," but my
hands kept patting themselves together. Besides, both my typewriters
were laid up.
    I wouldn't have had you change a thing about the "first" new
series issue, except that maybe you featured that guy Banks, whoever
he is, just a TAD (if I may use such language in a family publication)
too much.
    I certainly approve of the space given to a character created
by my favorite writer. Say, why don't you solicit another article by
Spillane authority Jim Traylor? The book he did in collaboration
with Max Collins was just enough to whet my appetite!
    The best single thing in your revival issue was the antiquarian
researches of Robert Sampson. May we hope for more?

From R.L. Wenstrup, 1045 Ten Mile Rd., New Richmond, OH 45157:

    What a treat to see MF back on schedule with my down-river
buddy alive and kicking, steeped once again in a mound of controversy!
    Guy, you must have a death wish. Either that or you have a
true-life mystery in the works: Who done it? Was it Bob ... Ellen
... Kathi ... Steve ... Jeff ...? The list of suspects boggles the mind.
    Regardless, MF remains the most **readable** rag of them all.
    P.S.--Better make that criminal law.
    **[Believe it or not--and I am perfectly well aware that a good
many will not--I don't go out and deliberately try to find contro-
versies in which to enmesh myself. The Napier brouhaha is a good
example of how I get into these things. Something happened in
the pages of Bob's letterzine which I felt was exceedingly important
to mystery fandom, of which I am a member. Because of the importance of what had happened, I tore myself away from other concerns
long enough to write to Bob about it. Bob refused to publish my
remarks--and the remarks of a great many other people. Because I
regarded the happening--the interjection of censorship into a mystery
publication--as something of great significance to mystery fandom,
I raised it in these pages as soon as I could. It received a lively
discussion in the following issue. The subject was brought out into
the open and every one was given the chance to give it the discussion**

it should have been given in Bob's magazine. Now that it has been discussed at length, I think that we can safely leave it behind and get on to other matters mysterious.

Not everyone agreed with me on the question--for which I am quite thankful (I'd hate to live in a world full of Guy Townsends-- or a room full, for that matter)--but I didn't bring the subject up for the purpose of being patted on the back. I brought it up because I believe that free discussion is essential to free thought. I brought it up because I believe that if one claims to be providing a forum for discussion, one has to be prepared to let the other side be heard as well. It should be clear to all by now that Bob's Mystery and Detection Monthly is not such a forum. And it should be equally clear that The Mystery Fancier long has been and continues to be just such a forum. So long as the opinions expressed are relevant, not libelous, and not too offensively obscene, they have a place in TMF, even if they are outrageous, obnoxious, and wrong-headed. That's as it should be, and as long as I am editing and publishing this rag that's the way it is going to be.]

From Otto Penzler, 129 West 56th St., New York, NY 10019:

With regard to your endless conversations with yourself about Bob Napier, and your one-dimensional political harangues: Stuff it. If you want to publish a politically-oriented fanzine, go ahead. But don't call it a mystery fiction fanzine.

[Q.E.D.]

The New Hard-Boiled Dicks: A Personal Checklist, by Robert E. Skinner--Volume Two in the Brownstone Chapbook Series--is now in production. The chapbook--which includes chapters on Andrew Bergman, James Crumley, Loren D. Estleman, Stephen Greenleaf, Donald Hamilton, Chester Himes, Stuart Kaminsky, Elmore Leonard, Robert B. Parker, Richard Stark (Donald E. Westlake), Jim Steranko, Ernest Tidyman, and others--will be approximately seventy pages long and is available directly from the publisher for $6.95, postpaid.

BROWNSTONE BOOKS
1711 Clifty Drive
Madison, Indiana 47250

www.ingramcontent.com/pod-product-compliance
Lightning Source LLC
Chambersburg PA
CBHW031435040426

42444CB00006B/824